New Construction for Older Buildings

A Design Sourcebook for Architects and Preservationists

Peter H. Smeallie

Peter H. Smith

A Wiley-Interscience Publication
John Wiley & Sons, Inc.
New York / Chichester / Brisbane / Toronto / Singapore

Library of Congress Cataloging in Publication Data:
Smeallie, Peter H.
    New construction for older buildings: a design sourcebook for
architects and preservationists / Peter H. Smeallie, Peter H. Smith.
        p.   cm.
    Bibliography: p.
    Includes index.
    1. Buildings—Remodeling for other use.   2. Buildings—Repair and
reconstruction.   3. Buildings—Conservation and restoration.

    I. Smith, Peter H.   II. Title.
    NA2793.S44   1989
    720′.28′6—dc20   89-16410
    ISBN 0-471-83134-4   CIP

Printed in the United States of America

10 9 8 7 6 5 4 3 2 1

To Holly,
Caroline,
Eleanor,
Peter

Contents

Foreword / viii
Preface / ix

I. ADDITIONS TO BUILDINGS   1

1. Respectfully Adding On / 3
2. Different Additions: Contrast and Abstraction / 15
3. Imitative Additions / 25

II. ALTERING THE ORIGINAL   35

4. New Homes in Old Buildings / 37
5. Conversion to Offices / 65
6. Conversion to Institutional Use / 93
7. Interior Spaces / 111

III. CONSTRUCTING ANEW AMID OLD   131

8. Freestanding Construction in Old Neighborhoods / 133
9. New Construction Attached to Old Buildings / 145
10. Retaining Facades / 157
11. Site and Urban Design / 169
12. The Missing Tooth: New Infill Construction / 189

Index to Professional Firms / 205
Subject Index / 207

Foreword

This book is a survey of architectural attitudes toward the existing built environment. The wide range in the quality of the work, from excellent to routine, might be expected, but the geographic range of these projects is surprising, as is the amount of work by "signature" architectural firms. The inclusion of examples by modern firms such as Roche Dinkeloo, SOM, Cambridge Seven Associates, Geddes Brecher Qualls Cunningham, and even Paul Rudolph is astonishing.

Also astonishing is the fact that a number of architectural firms have concentrated virtually their entire practice on designing with and around old buildings. Their influence on current practices of architecture is often very quiet and known only in a limited geographical area. Yet these firms prosper and have substantial impact on their localities.

The architectural profession gave the public fifty years of modern architecture, and the public responded with the greatest wave of architectural preservation in history. The work in this book illustrates the profession's response to the preservation movement. The architectural profession has now come to terms with the existing built environment and is dealing with it to the best of its ability.

The profession no longer needs to feel compelled to either reject past models or blindly embrace the past. What this work shows is that design decisions can and should combine a reasoned approach to the existing environment with the demands of today. The examples in this book illustrate the wide range of responses as well as varying degrees of success.

The intellectual battle for preservation has been won. What is needed now is more new work that is equal in quality to the work that is being preserved. This survey should help us all move closer to this common goal.

GEORGE E. HARTMAN

Washington, D.C.

Preface

"Something old, something new, something borrowed, and something blue." Like the good-luck items of the nervous bride-to-be, buildings are put together with the old, the new, the borrowed, and, often, the blue (although it may be "the blues" if you ask the designer). Creating new spaces near, next to, around, over, and even within old spaces is a challenge design professionals are facing more frequently and are responding to in innovative ways.

This book is about interesting architecture in the 1980s, viz., architecture that combines old and new buildings. Fostered in large part by the historic preservation movement, this mixing of new amid the old is no longer limited to historic or significant buildings. As many of the examples in this book show, it is also not limited to "old" buildings; relatively new buildings, constructed not more than a decade or two ago, have been combined with even newer buildings.

The benefits of combining old and new buildings are not lost on the architectural media. Awards are frequently given to projects that successfully integrate new with existing construction. A recent article on the subject stated that "Architects commissioned to renovate existing buildings have often merged old and new, producing a vibrant and positive result that has strengthened the old fabric of the city and enhanced our quality of life."[1]

The historic preservation movement should be credited with popularizing and making commonplace projects that mix old and new in this country. Tax incentives for rehabilitation projects have resulted in $12 billion spent on a massive number of projects (18,000) from 1976 to 1988.[2] Although less than consistent in practice and generally tied to the age and perceived historical significance of an existing building, these tax incentives have provided economic benefits that induced owners and developers to retain and use old buildings as part of their projects.

A number of other factors have fostered interest in reusing old buildings

[1] Webb Nichols, "Boston's Latest Building Boom Leaves Unsettling Results," *Boston Globe*, October 23, 1988, p. 90.
[2] Thomas Colin, "What Next for a Troubled Industry," *Historic Preservation*, May/June 1988, p. 32.

as parts of newer architectural projects. In many cities, landmark and historic district ordinances require developers to consider combining historic structures with new construction. In some cities, with strong local laws, developers are required to keep existing historic buildings as part of any new development plan.

For the most part, the examples are projects that have been constructed during the 1980s. For each example, we have tried to present the relevant background information on the structure involved and to stress how a particular problem was solved. Our emphasis is not as much on the aesthetic issues involved in combining old and new architecture as on the practical aspects of design work that must be confronted in such projects.

For example, parking requirements for automobiles and loading facilities for trucks are consistent threads that appear throughout the examples in the book. Interior circulation presents particular and constant problems. Systems integration—heating, ventilating, and air conditioning as well as joining structural systems—involves the constant creativity of engineers. Finally, how the identity of a new building is or is not maintained when combined with an existing structure is a challenge wrestled with by the project architect in many, if not most, of the examples.

Since this is not a historic preservation publication we use terms such as renovation, rehabilitation, remodeling, reuse, and adaptive use interchangeably. Although these terms have precise meanings to the professional historic preservationist, we believe that to the general public they convey basically the same meaning and that the precise nuances of their differences need not be grappled with in a work of this nature.

Aesthetic preference and community awareness are important factors that influence how old buildings are treated. There is a growing appreciation of the architectural embellishments and exuberance of historical styles of architecture. In 1989, J. Jackson Walter, president of the National Trust for Historic Preservation, reported membership at 225,000, up from 145,000 just four years earlier. The continuity from generation to generation represented by old buildings is a strong force. As one woman who became involved in historic preservation expressed it, she sensed a loss when "something fat and turreted" was torn down in her neighborhood.

There are as many ways to combine old and new buildings as there are old and new buildings. For clarity, this book is divided into three sections, each of which addresses an approach used in combining old and new architecture: (1) additions to buildings, (2) altering the original, and (3) new construction. Section I examines different design philosophies that are used when new space is added onto an existing building. Section II presents projects that combine old and new architecture for housing, office space, and institutional use. Interior changes, including retail uses, are also covered in this section. Finally, Section III, which covers new construction, shows how new buildings can be integrated into an existing context.

There are 12 chapters in this book, each consisting of a general introduction to the subject and a number of examples to illustrate different approaches to the same challenge. The examples chosen by the authors show how a particular problem involving combining old and new architecture has been solved; we believe that the projects contained in this book demonstrate the wealth of architectural talent currently being applied successfully in projects that combine old and new architecture.

We include examples that range in size from small residential buildings to large office and retail complexes. We have tried to include imaginative and innovative projects throughout the country to illustrate the universality of this type of architecture. Nevertheless, there are a number of examples from in and around Washington, D.C. The Washington metropolitan area has an established tradition in this area and has strong zoning as well as other requirements that developers must adhere to. In addition, the Washington area has undergone tremendous growth during the 1980s that has translated into a number of interesting and worthy projects.

Most of the examples included in the text were supplied to us by architects and designers throughout the country. We made two separate mail canvasses of architects around the nation to solicit projects. We were extremely pleased with the number and quality of responses received. We wish to thank all those who took the time and effort to answer our queries and to help us to understand the projects.

We owe a number of people a special thank you. Tom Vonier, AIA, provided advice, guidance, and direction at any number of points in the project. Katharine Smeallie, Gretchen Bank, and Stephen Figliozzi provided us with considerable assistance during the discovery phase of writing the book. Delphine Glaze was always on call to assist us with the manuscript preparation. To each of you, our thanks.

PETER H. SMEALLIE
PETER H. SMITH

Alexandria, Virginia
Washington, District of Columbia
February 1990

ADDITIONS TO BUILDINGS

Additions to buildings constitute the most frequent and important occurrences of mixing old and new architecture. The new architecture—the addition—poses a challenge to the project designer: how to create a new structure that is physically linked and functionally connected to an existing building. This challenge of mixing existing and new elements is evident in site considerations, design themes, circulation, and mechanical/electrical integration—in short, the entire range of building considerations.

For purposes of this section, an addition is defined as a construction project that is physically connected to an existing structure as distinct from alterations or freestanding new construction. An addition implies improvement; its Latin root, *dare*, means *to give*. An addition gives more space and more room to carry out the building's functions.

David R. Dibner and Amy Dibner-Dunlap in their book, *Building Additions Design*, indicate that a number of factors have contributed to an increase in building additions as a percentage of overall construction activity during the last decade. These include the high cost of new construction, the inherent energy conserving features of many older, existing buildings, and, not insignificantly, the "increasing desire of many informed people to save the physical evidence of our heritage in the form of architecturally and historically significant buildings."[1]

Additions are carried out for a variety of reasons, but in all cases, it is the need for additional space that motivates the expansion. Additions may be constructed because building a separate facility away from the main building is neither economic (e.g., in the case of a factory) nor desirable (e.g., an art museum). A common reason for additions is to create new space that will allow the older building to meet the demands of the twentieth century, such

[1] David R. Dibner, FAIA, and Amy Dibner-Dunlap, *Building Additions Design*, New York: McGraw-Hill, Inc., 1985, p. xi.

1

as improved access for the handicapped or for fire safety, space for modern mechanical and electrical systems, and computer needs and requirements.

Often an existing building cannot be successfully modified to meet these new requirements. For example, ceilings may be too high or too low to allow modifications. In many instances, an existing building itself represents an important asset in terms of location, image, or investment. An addition to such a building is a virtual necessity.

Additions can take many forms and configurations. Dibner and Dunlap describe horizontal additions, vertical additions, linked additions, modular expansion, natural growth, internal expansion, and additions as enclosures.[2] The discussion here is limited to the more traditional type of additions, that is, additions in which the expansion takes place in a horizontal direction on the existing or on an adjacent site.

The first three chapters of this book address additions from three design approaches. Chapter 1 examines additions that are appreciative and respectful of the original structure, Chapter 2 discusses additions as contrasting architectural statements to the original structure, and Chapter 3 looks at additions that duplicate or imitate the old building.

[2] Ibid., pp. 12–28.

1

Respectfully Adding On

This chapter describes building additions that are appreciative of the original structure in design approach, scale, materials, and other characteristics. Such additions are designed to stay consciously in the background and not to overwhelm the original building. This type of addition is intended to defer to the original building; it offers needed expansion without competing design goals. Even though such additions may be described as backdrop additions or deferential additions, they should not be relegated to second-class architecture. Appreciative additions respect the original building, but can offer such respect in noticeable ways.

An appreciative addition can be compared to a loyal corporate vice-president. Although both the president and vice-president may have the capability to perform the same functions as the leader, a good appreciative addition, like a good vice-president, maintains a distinct character that respects the standards set by the leader. Appreciative additions remain in the background and do not attempt to upstage the main character in the public's mind.

Straining the analogy further, the original building must be like the president of the company—it should be a distinguished structure having a commanding presence or a strong visual bearing to require a respectful addition. If the original building does not have such attributes, another type of design approach should be considered.

Most historic buildings or buildings that are local or national landmarks will be served best by appreciative additions. These buildings are often legally protected or are held in such high regard by the community that the addition's designers should make every effort not to detract from or interfere with the building's original design intent. Many organizations that are housed in important historic or community buildings choose appreciative additions because of the importance the organization attaches to the original building. For example, if an addition is contemplated for a distinguished state capitol or city hall, an appreciative addition is usually the appropriate solution.

Because appreciative additions are frequently made to buildings of historic importance, such additions are more likely than others to be subject to a design review process by a local landmarks commission or a historic district review board. In such cases, the exterior design of the addition will be subject to intense public scrutiny and criticism. Accordingly, designers should first make a thorough study and analysis of the design features and characteristics of the existing building before beginning any design studies for an addition.

The first rule in developing an appreciative or respectful addition is that the new portion not detract from the original structure, that is, the original building should continue to present the primary image. For example, in a unified streetscape of prominent buildings, additions should respect the streetscape. The principal design response in such instances is often to locate the building behind the existing structure rather than alongside it.

A particularly interesting example of such an approach is found along the north side of Constitution Avenue in Washington, D.C., between 17th and 23rd Streets. There, a number of large, freestanding early twentieth-century Beaux-Arts buildings housing important national organizations are set well back from the street on manicured lawns that face the Mall. As these organizations have expanded, they have inevitably required additional space.

One such organization, the National Academy of Sciences, added east and west wings and an auditorium in 1962, 1965, and 1970, respectively. These additions were carefully designed to achieve a symmetry that would be sympathetic to the original Beaux-Arts plan. The additions are not visible from the front—the Constitution Avenue side—but filled in open areas of the Academy's site on the sides and rear of the building.

The exterior design of the additions retains the original design motif using the same stone work patterns and window trim designs. However, there are distinctions. For example, "The wings' exterior doors match [Bertram] Goodhue's [the original architect] in size; like his, they have eight panels, but unlike his they lack decoration. Prometheus and Athena, frequently represented in the original building's decoration, appear on the interior and exterior handles on the west wing doors."[3]

Many excellent examples of appreciative additions to important buildings can be found throughout the United States. Although the exterior, visual elements of an appreciative addition are usually the most salient features, factors other than design are often the key to a successful addition. The functional fit between the old and new is extremely important.

Circulation patterns should be considered carefully so that people can move easily from one section of the building to another. There is not always an obvious or easy solution to this problem. Because of changes in standard construction techniques during this century, standard floor levels between a nineteenth-century building and a contemporary addition may not match. Although the transition between the various grade levels can be handled in a number of ways, in many types of buildings, such as hospitals, it is often the crucial factor in adding a new portion. Similarly, changes and advances in heating and cooling technology can create different environments between an old building and its newer addition if there is not adequate consideration given to the HVAC system.

The choice of building materials is an important element in planning appreciative additions, since normally facade materials that are similar to or the same as that of the main structure are used. Although cost considerations are

[3] National Academy of Sciences, *A Temple of Science*, Washington, D.C.: National Academy Press, 1984, p. 33.

The west wing of the National Academy of Sciences, built in 1962, uses the same exterior material as the original, the side facade of which is partially visible in the right of the photo. Photographic credit: National Academy of Sciences.

The Academy building's location in ceremonial Washington, D.C. required appreciative architecture for each of its three additions. The auditorium addition, built in 1970, is in the foreground, the west wing to the right, and the east wing—similar to the west wing—is obscured by the larger auditorium addition. Photographic credit: Robert Lautman.

A major addition to the historic Newberry Library in Chicago, Illinois, provides environmentally sound new space in which to preserve the valuable resources of the library. The new addition has no windows to prevent the introduction of harmful sunlight. Detailing on the exterior of the addition and the use of similar facade materials clearly indicate that the two structures are related. Photographic credit: Peter H. Smeallie.

an important factor in the choice of exterior materials, attempts should be made to respect the original choice of building materials in an appreciative addition.

The transition between the old portion and the new addition is perhaps the most prominent feature of many additions to existing buildings. The architect must pay particular attention to the connection between the old building and the new addition. If poorly handled, the connection can distort the design quality of both portions of the building and can lead to major circulation problems between the two. When skillfully handled, the connection serves as a logical transition zone that demarcates where one part ends and the other begins.

Characteristics of architectural style are crucial in achieving a successful appreciative addition. For example, the tripartite form of a Beaux-Arts building should be reflected in an appreciative addition. Similarly, the symmetry found in Federal-style buildings should be evident. The designer of an appreciative addition must be conscious of other stylistic attributes such as window and door placement, rhythm and roof lines, and pitch.

The relationship of the scale of the addition to the original building is an important design consideration. An appreciative addition normally attempts to emulate the height and bulk of the original, without overwhelming it. However, this is not always the case. In situations in which extensive amounts of additional space are required, respectful additions can be considerably larger than the original building. For example, museums and libraries may require the addition of space that is several times larger than was originally constructed.

In such instances, very large additions may be an entirely appropriate response. For example, in Chicago, Illinois, the historically significant Newberry Library, built in 1891 and designed by Henry Ives Cobb, required an addition that was greater in size than the original library building to house its expanding collections. At the same time, requirements for the conservation of fragile library resources and materials dictated greatly expanded HVAC capabilities for the entire library. The new addition was designed in 1982 by Harry Weese and Associates to achieve all these needs. The goals were met by developing a large new addition that created a windowless box that was respectful of the historical importance of the Newberry Library's original building through the use of materials and architectural detailing.

Creating New Space in a Monumental Building

The Folger Shakespeare Library, located on Capitol Hill in Washington, D.C., houses one of the world's most important collections of Shakespearean material. The building was designed in 1928–1932 by Paul Cret in a curvilinear Beaux-

A new addition to the Folger Shakespeare Library in Washington, D.C. houses a new reading room and storage areas for the institution. The new addition, which is not visible from the street, fills in the U between the wings of the 1932 building using similar facade materials. The new addition is suspended over the parking area to allow access. Photographic credit: Cervin Robinson.

CREDITS
NAME AND LOCATION: Folger Shakespeare Library, Washington, D.C.
ARCHITECTS: Hartman-Cox Architects, Washington, D.C.

Arts style. As the collection of the library has grown, so too has its scholarly patronage. By about the mid-1970s, it had become apparent that additional space was necessary to accommodate the increased demands.

A new reading room for the library was added by placing the new space in the center of a U between two wings at the rear of the building. The addition, which is not visible from the street, uses the same exterior facade materials that are evident on the original building. To allow continued access to the building's parking facilities, the architects literally suspended the addition from a steel frame that spans the parking bays to tie into the original footings.

The addition, with its new reading room and library storage areas, incorporates a new HVAC system to supplement the original HVAC system. The addition won a 1988 AIA Honor Award.

Appreciative Residential Addition

The Cartney-Hunt House in Columbus, Mississippi is a Federal-style, brick structure. When the owners decided to expand the house to develop a tourist bed and breakfast facility, more room was needed. The addition created the necessary space by placing the addition at the rear of the house to preserve

The addition to the rear of the Cartney-Hunt House in Columbus, Mississippi, follows the architectural lines of the original Federal style structure.

CREDITS
NAME AND LOCATION: Cartney-Hunt House, Columbus, Mississippi
ARCHITECT: Samuel H. Kaye, AIA, Architect, Columbus, Mississippi

the historic streetscape. The architectural style of the addition was carried out in the same Federal style and materials as the original building.

Chrysler Museum Renovation

In 1971 the Norfolk (Virginia) Museum of Arts and Sciences was the beneficiary of a considerable collection of art from Walter Chrysler; the museum changed its name to reflect its benefactor and added a wing to house the collection. The addition of the 1970s wing, along with a wing that was built in the 1960s, and a generally confusing floor layout led to a plan to make sense of the hodgepodge of architectural styles and maze of interior spaces. The director, David Steadman, described the museum as a place with "no central space and no large galleries in three unrelated buildings with the wrong site orientation and the entrance on the wrong side."[4]

The architects renewed the museum by adding a new wing that was similar to the 1960s wing, hiding the brutal 1970s wing, adding an identical tower, refacing the structure to match the original museum building, and opening

A major renovation of the Chrysler Museum in Norfolk, Virginia includes a reorientation of the museum's interior layout as well as a new wing. The new wing and tower are similar in style and materials to the original architectural character of the structure. Photographic credit: Peter Aaron, Esto Photographics, Inc.

CREDITS
NAME & LOCATION: Chrysler Museum, Norfolk, Virginia
ARCHITECT: Hartman-Cox Architects, Washington, D.C.

[4] Benjamin Forgey, "The Chrysler Museum, Suddenly Splendid," *The Washington Post*, February 26, 1989, p. G1.

The central wing of the Greenbrier Resort in White Sulphur Springs, West Virginia was completed in 1910 and designed in a Georgian Revival style. Three additional wings were added in 1930, and there have been a number of subsequent additions. All have continued the Georgian Revival style tradition. The continuity of architecture reflects the continuity of the resort.

Resort Hotel Adds Through the Years

The Greenbrier Resort in White Sulphur Springs, West Virginia is one of the most famous resort complexes in the country. Its history as a medicinal bath dates from 1778. The complex that currently houses all the various activities of the resort was begun in 1910. The first element, a 250-room Georgian Revival structure, was designed by New York architect Frederick Junius Sterner. This structure is currently the central wing of the resort.

Three additional wings were added in 1930. Designed by the Cleveland architectural firm of Small, Smith and Webb, the new additions reproduced the Georgian Revival architecture of the original center wing. Other wings and facilities were added in 1954, 1962, and 1974, all continuing the tradition of Georgian Revival style design.

The hotel has also undergone a number of upgradings and modernizations, all of which have made conscious efforts to maintain the sense of architectural continuity and design. The architectural style of the Greenbrier is a means of creating respect for the history of the resort as well as an excellent marketing tool.

up interior spaces to align with the original plan of the museum. This example shows that appreciative additions can go beyond a "new wing" and can, in similar eclectic situations, transform an embarrassing architectural pile-up into a respected piece of the urban landscape.

New Carriage House Addition

Decatur House is located in Washington, D.C.'s Lafayette Square across the street from the White House. It is a property of the National Trust for Historic Preservation. The original building, built in 1818–1819, was designed by Benjamin Henry Latrobe and the complex includes a number of outbuildings dating from the mid-nineteenth century. In 1986, an addition to the Carriage House was completed and is used as a reception and program area for the museum property.

The addition respects the character of the historic property by using materials that match the nineteenth-century wings added to the main structure. It maintains the historic roof line and pitch, as well as the symmetry of the historic architecture. The addition creates modern functional space that was needed to support the museum functions and operations of the historic property. The addition does not attempt to compete with the neoclassical architecture of the main structure; it is intended to improve the appearance of the garden and historic courtyard of the property.

This axonometric view of the revitalized Decatur Carriage House in Washington, D.C. illustrates how the roof line and pitch of the original historic structures were maintained. Decatur House is a property of the National Trust for Historic Preservation. Drawing: McCartney Lewis Architects.

CREDITS
NAME & LOCATION: Decatur Carriage House, Washington, D.C.
ARCHITECT: McCartney Lewis Architects, Washington, D.C.
DEVELOPER: National Trust for Historic Preservation, Washington, D.C.

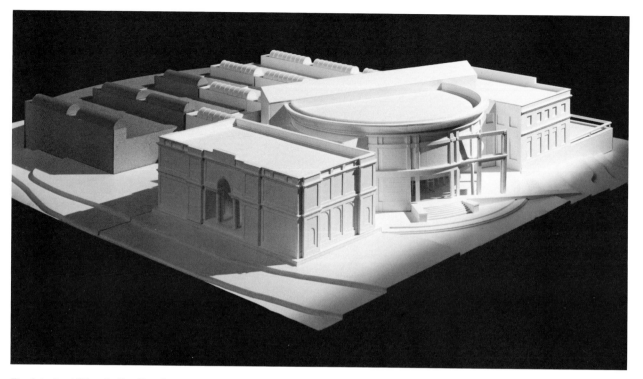

The latest addition to the Brooks Museum of Art in Memphis, Tennessee provides new links between the central block of the main 1915 gallery and several subsequent additions as well as providing new support facilities for the museum. Model photography: Joe Aker.

CREDITS
NAME AND LOCATION: Brooks Museum of Art, Memphis, Tennessee
ARCHITECTS: Skidmore, Owings & Merrill, Houston, Texas

New Addition to the Brooks Museum of Art

The original portion of the Brooks Museum of Art, located in Memphis, Tennessee, was designed by James Gamble Rogers and built in Overton Park in 1915. Additions were built in 1955 and 1973. Plans developed in 1987 by Skidmore, Owings & Merrill called for an addition that provided a central block to link the original structure with the galleries housed in the 1973 addition as well as a dining facility, the museum shop, additional gallery spaces, and support areas. The design of the latest addition respects the facade delineation of the original building. The new plan will create two main entrances, one for groups and the other for the general public to allow good circulation throughout the museum.

Willard Hotel

The Willard Hotel, designed by Henry Hardenbergh and built in 1901–1904, has been called the "residence of Presidents" due to its prominent location and status in Washington, D.C. The hotel was closed in 1968, and, after a lengthy legal battle, was purchased by the Pennsylvania Avenue Development Corporation, a federal agency charged with bringing back to life "the nation's main street." The idea for the addition, which made possible the restoration of the grand old hotel, was developed by the New York architectural firm of Hardy Holzman Pfeiffer and was carried out by Vlastimil Koubek of Washington. The addition to the hotel serves as office space for many national and international firms desiring an office address on Pennsylvania Avenue. The ground floor of the new section houses retail boutiques and restaurants.

The design of the addition uses the motifs of the mansard roofs of the Second Empire style that are such a prominent feature of the Willard in a

The addition to the historic Willard Hotel, Washington, D.C., which houses offices, shops, and restaurants, uses similar mansard roof motifs and fenestration to create an appreciative addition. The new construction and addition is now the Willard Inter-Continental Hotel and the Willard Office Building. Photographic credit: The Willard Inter-Continental.

CREDITS
NAME AND LOCATION: Willard Inter-Continental Hotel and the Willard Office Building, Washington, D.C.
ARCHITECTS: Hardy, Holzman, and Pfeifer, New York, New York; Vlastimil Koubek, Washington, D.C.
DEVELOPER: Oliver Carr Company, Washington, D.C., and Stuart Golding
OWNER: Willard Associates, Washington, D.C.

---

manner that clearly ties the addition to the original building. Although the details are drawn from the original hotel, the shape and form of the office addition are different, but entirely appreciative of the original. The addition is in four stepped sections, and the entire section is angled off from the street, creating a deferential set back for the Willard and providing a public space on the nation's most public street.

The addition is joined to the hotel via a connecting archway that creates a passageway through the interior of the block from Pennsylvania Avenue to F Street, a main shopping street of downtown Washington.

2

Different Additions: Contrast and Abstraction

Whereas an appreciative addition focuses attention on the original building, other types of additions complement the original building, but stand out in their own right. Two of these addition styles are contrast and abstraction.[1] Contrasting additions use opposing colors, forms, and other design elements in a manner that, if successfully applied, heightens the effect of the whole. Abstract additions use design elements that are apart, but representative, of the original.

A contrasting addition emphasizes the separate architectural styles of the original and the addition. An abstract addition alludes to and makes use of existing design elements without any attempt to recreate them. It summarizes the qualities of the original design in a manner that is connected only loosely to the original design intent.

With these types of additions, all of the major planning considerations required of appreciative additions are present. That is, the designer must carefully consider connectors between the old and new portions of the building, mechanical and engineering integration, as well as functional, access, circulation, and other requirements.

The primary distinction between appreciative additions and contrasting or abstract additions is one of architectural style. A contrasting or abstract addition is a very visible part of the entire building. Unlike an appreciative addition, it does not seek background status; such an addition seeks the foreground, drawing attention to itself and its contribution to the overall structure.

In stylistic terms, a contrasting addition quickly and clearly defines what

[1] Keith Ray (ed.), *Contextual Architecture: Responding to Existing Style*, New York: McGraw-Hill, Inc., 1980.

15

part of the building is the addition. For example, adding a postmodern addition to a Beaux-Arts style building or a curtain wall addition to a colonial revival structure would present sharp contrasting architectural styles.

Contrasting building materials are often used. For example, an addition of a glass facade onto a red brick building would present a material markedly different from the original structure. Color schemes can clearly contrast the old and new. For example, different colors of the same material are often used to highlight the new addition. A contrasting addition can also be achieved by greatly varying the scale. For example, a four- or five-story building could have a 10- or more story addition attached to it.

It is difficult to put precise definitional boundaries on abstraction in building additions. For example, an abstract addition may use the original building's proportions and vary other design elements. Or an addition's height and massing may vary significantly and distinctly from the original, relying on other elements to tie the addition back to the original structure. Exaggerating or enlarging certain design elements of the original in the addition can create an addition that makes use of the original design elements, but is also an abstraction.

Another design technique used in abstract additions is to elongate a particular design element, using materials that are similar to, but clearly different from, the original materials, such as bricks that are substantially different in size from common brick.

The use of contrast or abstraction in a building addition is intended to draw attention to the new addition, and to make a statement about the building's development, history, image, and uses. These additions are not intended to be respectful or deferential to the existing building, but are often intended to provide new meanings or associations about the building. Nevertheless, con-

A contrasting addition was added to McKim, Mead and White's 1895 Boston Public Library in Boston, Massachusetts by the New York architectural firm of Johnson/Burgee in 1973. The new addition, while maintaining the scale of the original building, has a rough concrete facade that contrasts with the polished granite facade of the 1985 structure.
Photographic credit: Fay Foto, Inc., Boston, Massachusetts.

trasting and abstract additions draw their fundamental design cues from the existing building.

In both contrasting and abstract additions, the prevailing style, materials, and color of the existing building are used as foils to develop a new design approach. Many projects successfully merge both contrast and abstraction in a single addition. One of the best known examples is the addition to the Boston Public Library on Copley Square. The original building was designed in a classical Beaux-Arts style by McKim, Mead and White and completed in 1895. The library expanded in 1973 with an addition designed by Johnson/Burgee Architects.

The addition uses the design clues of the original building as its starting point. The rough form concrete material of the facade of the new addition contrasts sharply with the smooth, polished granite surface of the original building. The scale of the addition, with its large bays and simply detailed, widely arched openings contrasts sharply with the more intimate scale of the original with its smaller bays, richly ornamented detailing, and narrow, arched windows. The details of the addition such as the arched doorways and window openings are abstractions of those originally designed by McKim, Mead and White.

Contrasting and abstract additions present intriguing and, at times, conflicting design challenges. These types of additions are essentially an intellectualization of the intent of the original designer. As such, they require the designer to understand fully the purpose, intent, and use of the existing building as envisioned by the original designer. Contrasting and abstract additions must respect the style and intent of the original building to be successful; otherwise, the addition risks becoming a parody that will not achieve its intended purpose.

Historical Society Gets Wrap-Around Addition

What began for the Chicago Historical Society as a quest for more storage space for the museum's collections ended up as a major addition to the building that, in turn, reordered the collections, the exhibits, the staff, and the visitor's experience. The original building of the Chicago Historical Society, a red brick Georgian Revival building in Lincoln Park, was built in 1932.

In 1971, a new front wing was added to the museum. This addition, in a Classical style with limestone facing, was not popular, created identity problems for the museum, and ended up being labeled by the director of the museum as "neo-Fascist."[2] By 1981, it was clear that the museum needed extensive additional space (up to 50,000 square feet) in which to house its collection.

The museum's original idea was to house the additional space below grade. However, design consultants recommended that the bulk of the addition (all but 15,000 square feet) be built above grade. The new addition involves encasing and wrapping the 1971 addition with new construction that redefines the museum's entryway, renovates gallery space in both the 1932 portion and the 1971 portion, and adds a connecting element between the two existing sections of the building.

An important consideration in the design of the new wrap-around addition and the new connector was to preserve both the original Georgian Revival building and the park land surrounding the museum. New space had to be contained within the existing outline of the structure. The wrap-around addition

[2] Margaret Doyle, "Chicago Historical Society," *Building Design and Construction*, October 1988, p. 50.

A new addition to the Chicago Historical Society wraps around an earlier addition to create expanded space for collections, exhibitions, storage and staff. Photographic credit: Lambros Photography.

CREDITS
NAME & LOCATION: Chicago Historical Society, Chicago, Illinois
ARCHITECT: Holabird and Root Architects, Gerald Horn, Designer, Chicago, Illinois

The principal facade of the addition on Clark Street is marked by a large, open pedimented steel truss to emphasize the major entryway into the museum. Photographic credit: David Clifton.

A new connector was created between the original 1931 Georgian Revival building and a 1971 Classical revival addition. The connector uses a large gabled steel-framed glass window as part of new atrium space. Photographic credit: David Clifton.

follows the perimeter lines of the 1932 building and wraps around the visible sides of the 1971 addition.

The design of the addition uses a brick facade that echoes the material of the original building. A large, open, pedimented steel truss marks the major entranceway into the museum. A curvilinear corner of white structural steel and a gridded window wall is located at the southern end. On the ground level, floor-to-ceiling windows provide display space and a glimpse of the museum store. The second floor of the new addition is windowless; the third floor includes windows for staff offices.

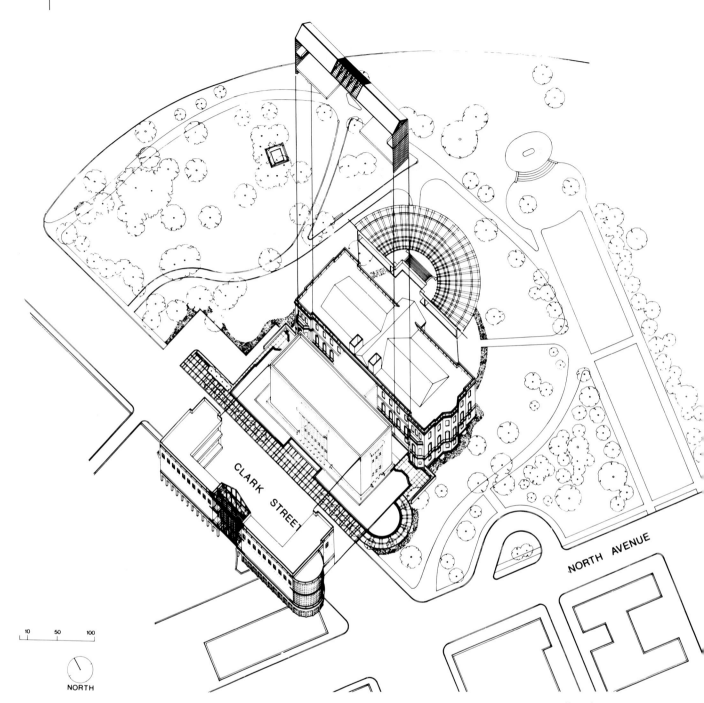

The new addition to the museum does not intrude into the park surrounding the museum. Storage space is located beneath a new plaza that will be used as a performance and ceremonial space by the museum. Drawing credit: Holabird and Root.

The facade of the new connector between the main components also uses a large gabled steel-framed glass window wall with mullions to create new atrium space. The fenestration of the new addition is designed to match that of the 1932 building. A new storage area is located to the east of the original building underneath a new plaza, which will serve as a ceremonial area for museum functions and a transition zone between the adjacent park and the museum building.

The extensive additions and renovations require three mechanical systems—two for the new building and one for the storage area. The boilers and chillers of the original building provide the supply to these new mechanical systems. In addition, supplemental air conditioning had to be provided to the two new atrium galleries created by the large expanses of glass.

Reviving a Major Downtown Office Building

In downtown Oklahoma City, the Perrine Building, built in 1927, has been reborn, after much labor, as the Robinson Renaissance Building. The original structure was U-shaped, fronting on two downtown city blocks, and featured art deco detailing. The original light well between the two flanking wings of the building became a 12-story skylight and atrium roofed with glass. The

An addition to the former Perrine Building built in 1927 in downtown Oklahoma City, Oklahoma, has transformed the structure into the Robinson Renaissance Building. The building's original light well has been filled in with a skylight and atrium. Pedestrian walkways now connect the upper floors of the building. Photographic credit: HTB, Inc.

CREDITS
NAME AND LOCATION: Robinson Renaissance Building, Oklahoma City, Oklahoma
ARCHITECT: HTB, Inc., Director of Design: Larry J. Keller, Oklahoma City, Oklahoma

filled-in light well allowed the construction of pedestrian walkways between the two wings on the upper floors of the building. The ground floor space was rehabilitated to serve as retail space.

Addition on Top Creates More Room for Banking

A bank in the heart of the financial district in Washington, D.C. needed more room for operational needs for modern banking practices. The original building was built in 1907 in a classic Beaux-Arts style, and a substantial addition that matched the original was carried out in 1927.

To preserve the original building and extend the height of the building up to the maximum allowed by local zoning laws, the space of a rear courtyard was used. The visible portion of the addition on top of the building made use of the primary architectural elements of the historic building, which include the stark white color of the marble and granite facade and the rhythm created by the spacing of monumental columns. The new addition, barely visible from street level, is clearly modern in appearance, but maintains solid ties with the original building.

A contrasting addition on the top of the 1st American Bank Building, a beaux-arts building in Washington, D.C.'s financial district, provided additional room for its operations while maintaining the original structure. The addition, which makes use of the primary design elements of the historic building, is barely visible from the street.
Photographic credit: Gary Fleming.

CREDITS
NAME & LOCATION: 1st American Bank Building, Washington, D.C.
ARCHITECT: Keyes Condon Florance Architects, Washington, D.C.
OWNER: 1st American Bankshares, Washington, D.C.

The former Terminal Refrigerating and Warehousing Company in southwest Washington, D.C., is now the Washington Design Center. Photographic credit: Gary Fleming.

CREDITS
NAME & LOCATION: Washington Design Center, Washington, D.C.
ARCHITECT: Keyes Condon Florance Architects, Washington, D.C.
ASSOCIATED ARCHITECT: Bryant & Bryant
OWNER: The Merchandise Mart Corporation

The mirrored glass facade of the addition contrasts sharply with the plain brick facade of the original building. The addition emphasizes the change in use of the structure. Photographic credit: James Oesch Photography.

Refrigeration Building to Modern Design Center

A dramatic addition to a large brick warehouse building in Washington, D.C. that once housed a refrigeration company makes the building easily recognizable and clearly defines its new use as the home of the Washington Design Center. The addition of mirror glass contrasts sharply with the brick exterior of the original warehouse both in material and surface finish.

Architectural detailing, such as pilasters, window type, and rhythm, is clearly reflected in the addition. Although this detailing serves as a connecting link that illustrates that the two halves of the building are part of one use, the extreme differences in materials create a striking visual contrast, further emphasized by the placement of the entrance to the complex at the point at which the two halves of the building meet.

3

Imitative Additions

Another form of addition can be appropriate under certain circumstances. This type of addition, called imitative, faithfully reproduces the architecture of the original building. An imitative addition attempts to integrate the addition with the original so that the entire building is considered one entity. The original building is copied including architectural style, windows, height, bulk, color, and materials. In its most extreme, an imitative addition obscures the point at which the original leaves off and the new begins.

Imitative additions can be found on many historically important buildings. The architectural style and image that these buildings possess may demand that any addition retain or at least not disturb these qualities. For example, a banker may believe that the bank building conveys to the public a stability and permanence consistent with the goals of the bank. A new addition would be designed to portray itself through architecture in the same manner as the original. The addition to the Richardsonian-style Riggs Bank Building at 9th and F Streets, Northwest, in Washington, D.C., was done in an imitative style in the 1920s. Today, with the passage of 70 years, it is virtually impossible to distinguish between the old and the new.

An imitative addition may be undertaken to show respect for the work of a particularly prominent designer. Although such additions can be viewed as a form of flattery, an increasingly common reason for the design of an imitative addition is the result of stylistic direction on the part of historic preservation review boards. Similarly, projects that add to historic structures may use imitative additions as a means of complying with the requirements for Federal tax incentives that are available for rehabilitated buildings.

Imitative additions are appropriate and are frequently the only form of addition undertaken on buildings for which the symbolic value of the structure is as important as the building itself. The most important example is that of the United States Capitol. A number of additions have been made to the building since the beginning of the nineteenth century. The last large addition was the expansion of the east front of the building in the 1950s. Each of the

The addition to a bank building in Washington, D.C. illustrates how seamless an imitative addition can be. The original building was built in 1901; the addition was completed in 1926. Photographic credit: Peter H. Smith.

additions has been careful to respect the architecture, design, and heritage of this symbol of American democracy.

An imitative addition would be appropriate on an unfinished historically or symbolically important structure. Other buildings may be designed to accommodate further expansion, where the appropriate design response would be an addition done in the style of the original. In some cases, an image conveyed by the building's architecture may be so distinctive or idiosyncratic that it virtually compels the design for an addition that reproduces the original style.

Too often, however, imitative additions are used as an excuse for poor architecture. For example, a Federal-style bank building adds a drive-in teller window in an imitative style or an addition of a parking garage to a Victorian department store is made to look like part of the store. An extreme example of an inappropriate imitative style occurred with the construction of the Yale University Harkness Tower in 1918. To authenticate the age of the newly constructed Gothic-style tower, the stone steps were delivered to the construction site already worn down. This misuse of imititative work landed the Harkness Tower in the book of *Star-Spangled Kitsch.*[1] Contemporary designs that are compatible with the original should be used in such cases.

Imitative additions are often small and serve as a means of providing new or improved services to the original structure. Such additions are meant to blend with the original building in an almost seamless fashion. For example, installing an elevator and fire stair for improved access to historic buildings is a common reason for designing imitative additions. Similarly, the installation

[1] Curtis F. Brown, *Star-Spangled Kitsch*, New York: Universe Books, 1975, p. 94.

of a new HVAC system that requires exterior ductwork is often done using a design that duplicates the original. Improvements of this type are done in an imitative manner precisely so that they do not draw attention to themselves and thereby detract from the architecture of the existing building.

There are any number of practical concerns that must be taken into account in carrying out imitative additions. The availability of the same building materials found in the original building as well as the necessary craftsmanship to construct the additions are two important constraints. For example, nominal material sizes have changed over the past century. Bricks today may not be the same standard size as bricks used for a nineteenth-century building. In such cases, either the brick size that most closely approximates the old size can be used in the construction or bricks can be specially ordered to conform to the exact specifications of the existing brick. Cost clearly plays a role in the determination of which approach is taken.

To produce an addition that precisely imitates the original, the designer must be conscious of matching the color between the old and the new portion of the structure. Facade color of buildings can change over time due to a number of factors such as pollutants. With brick or stone buildings, it is advisable that the surface of the original structure be thoroughly cleaned before determining the color match of the new material. Decades of accumulated grime can change the intended appearance of a building. New materials combined with newly cleaned surfaces will acquire a patina at the same rate so that, over time, their appearance will remain similar.

The east front of the United States Capitol. Photographic credit: Peter H. Smith.

Addition Allows Conversion of Armory into Mixed Use Arts Facility

In Hyattsville, Maryland a granite replica of England's Windsor Castle that was originally built in 1918 as an armory became, with imaginative site programming, the Castle Center for the Arts. The distinctive architectural style of the original facility almost demanded an addition that would copy the fortress-like architecture. The program called for the development of a 300-seat professional theater, a restaurant, as well as office and retail space. The lobby for the theater is located in a new addition in the loading dock area of the original armory building. The new addition incorporates a special mortar mix, split-faced block, and cast stone to simulate the original granite facade

The Castle Arts Center in Hyattsville, Maryland was originally built as an armory in 1918 to imitate Windsor Castle. An imaginative reuse plan converted the armory into a local arts center that includes a theater, restaurant, and office and retail space. Photographic credit: William Lebovich.

CREDITS
NAME AND LOCATION: Castle Center for the Arts, Hyattsville, Maryland
ARCHITECT: Mary L. Oehrlein, AIA, Oehrlein & Associates, Washington, D.C.

The addition to the rear of the Castle Arts Center uses rusticated stone and block to create an impression of the original facade of the building. Photographic credit: William Lebovich.

of the building. The design includes stylized buttresses and crenellations to imitate the architecture of the armory.

Because of the extraordinary mix of uses in the building, the mechanical and electrical systems presented exceptional challenges. A central heating system was considered too expensive for the facility. The solution was to use a tenant-controlled heat pump system tied to predetermined leasable segments of the building.

Architectural Style Determines Style of Residential Condominium Addition

In Denver, Colorado a French Mediterranean-style mansion built in 1911 by gold and silver baron Guilford S. Wood served as the design focus of a 26-unit residential condominium development. The mansion, named the Bonfils Mansion for one of its former residents, was, stylistically, considerably different than other mansions built by Denver's new rich in the latter part of the nineteenth century. Because of its rather unusual style of architecture, the building set the tone for the condominium development that surrounds and is attached to the original structure. The Mediterranean style and scale of the mansion is echoed in the design of the new units through the stucco exterior, tile roofs, French doors, and arched window openings. The reuse of the mansion includes three residential units as well as common meeting rooms and an exercise facility in the original basement. The project received an Award of Merit for Historic Preservation and Rehabilitation from the Denver chapter of the American Institute of Architects.

The Bonfils Mansion in Denver, Colorado was built in 1911 in a French Mediterranean style. The mansion is now the centerpiece of a condominium development (Encore Condominium Redevelopment, Denver, Colorado). Photographic credit: H.W.H. Associates, Inc.

CREDITS
NAME AND LOCATION: Encore Condominium Redevelopment, Denver, Colorado
ARCHITECT: H.W.H. Associates, Inc.; Daniel J. Havekost, FAIA, Principal in Charge, Denver, Colorado

The mansion's architectural style served as the determining factor for the design of the condominium development that was built on the former grounds of the mansion. Drawing credit: H.W.H. Associates, Inc.

Addition Preserves Museum's Identity

Since 1947 the Jewish Museum has occupied the Warburg Mansion on Manhattan's Upper East Side. The mansion was designed by C.P.H. Gilbert and built in 1907. The distinctive chateauesque style of the building has forged an identity for the museum in a neighborhood of other prominent museums including the Whitney and the Guggenheim. The need for additional gallery

The Jewish Museum in New York, New York is housed in the 1907 Warburg Mansion. A new addition to the museum virtually replicates the distinctive chateauesque style of building and makes clear that its landmark architecture is an important part of the identity of the museum. Drawing credit: Kevin Roche John Dinkeloo and Associates.

CREDITS
NAME AND LOCATION: Jewish Museum, New York, New York
ARCHITECTS: Kevin Roche John Dinkeloo and Associates, Hamden, Connecticut

and office space served as the impetus for the museum's desire to expand its facilities. The architect for the new addition is Kevin Roche, whose proposal for the wholly imitative addition to the Jewish Museum makes clear that the visual identity of the museum's landmark home is an extremely important aspect of the urban fabric of Manhattan.

Stair Tower for Former Hospital

An early twentieth-century hospital in Sioux Falls, South Dakota was completely remodeled in the early 1980s for modern office space. The reuse of the building as a law office included not only remodeling the interior of the structure but installing an exterior stair tower for access between the floors of the four-story

The stair tower addition to this former hospital in Sioux Falls, South Dakota matches the existing brick work to look as if it had always been part of the building.

CREDITS
NAME AND LOCATION: Davenport, Evans, Hurwitz & Smith Building, Sioux Falls, South Dakota
ARCHITECT: Steven M. Larson, Design Concepts, Inc., Sioux Falls, South Dakota

The new elevator tower for the Historical Society of Washington, D.C. blends with the finishes of the society's romanesque headquarters building. Photographic credit: Peter H. Smith.

CREDITS
NAME AND LOCATION: Historical
    Society of Washington, D.C.
ARCHITECT: Geier, Renfrow, Brown,
    Washington, D.C.

structure. The stair tower faithfully copied the existing finishes of the old structure and used matching brick work. From the exterior, it is difficult to discern where the old structure leaves off and the recent addition begins.

Mansion Gets Elevator Tower

The Historical Society of Washington, D.C. is housed in the Heurich Mansion, an opulent, Romanesque mansion built in the late nineteenth century and located in the DuPont Circle area of the city. In 1988 an exterior elevator tower was added to the building to improve access. The various facades of the building have considerably different detailing. The principal facade is faced with brownstone whereas the less important facades are faced in brick. The elevator tower is located on the north side of the building, one of the less prominent facades. The design of the elevator tower imitates the brick finish of the north side of the structure. From the exterior, this modern addition appears to be an integral part of the original mansion.

ALTERING THE ORIGINAL

It is estimated that 90 percent of all the buildings that will be in use at the end of this century are already built. As the nation's buildings become older—there are more than 500,000 buildings listed on the National Register of Historic Places—the chances for a change in use or a significant alteration become greater.

It is no longer the exception when a building is altered for a new use. In the foreword to *Remaking America*, Paul Goldberger writes:

> *It is no longer a radical idea to talk of saving older buildings, no longer an odd viewpoint to suggest that in many old buildings there may be whole new lives waiting to begin, and that these lives may even turn out to be more profitable economically than the building's previous ones.*[1]

This section examines how alterations to older buildings can change the use of the building to create new homes, new offices, and new spaces for institutions such as colleges and universities. Because many of the alterations take place on the interior of a structure, we include a chapter that examines new interiors in older buildings.

---

[1] Barbaralee Diamonstein, *New Uses, Old Places: Remaking America*, New York: Crown Publishers, Inc., 1986, p. 9.

4

New Homes in Old Buildings

As the demographic and economic bases of the nation change so do the types of buildings. The demographic "blip" caused by the baby boom generation, now at home-buying ages, has created a strong demand for housing of all types. The industrial age of the late nineteenth and early twentieth centuries demanded factory buildings for the manufacture of goods. The information age of today, powered by computers, demands a considerably different building type. The result is that there are thousands of buildings that have outlived their original economic purpose and have been converted to new uses.

Many single-purpose structures can no longer serve the economic function for which they were originally built. For example, textile mills in New England became obsolete when the center of the industry shifted to the sunbelt states. Now textile factories of the South are following the same pattern as textile manufacturing moves overseas leaving behind still more obsolete and under-utilized buildings.

Population shifts can occur in response to a regional recession in one area of the country and a strong economy in another. Such shifts can create a housing crunch in one region and a glut in another. Increasingly large numbers of people are concentrated in urban areas, necessitating a change in the style and size of housing. For example, it is costly to provide detached, single-family residential structures in densely developed urban areas.

As a result of these trends, a large inventory of unused or underutilized buildings exists with a similarly great demand for housing in many regions of the country. This chapter describes how these older, underused buildings have been converted for residential use. It will examine factors that must be considered when contemplating the reuse of an old building for housing. Although it does not describe proper techniques for restoring a house, the chapter attempts to set forth the steps that have to be taken to put old buildings to modern residential use.

Location is the major factor in the reuse of older buildings for housing. Convenience of location plays an important role as a great number of urban workers wish to live near where they work. This has made buildings in central city areas especially desirable as housing stock. Unused or underused buildings convenient to amenities such as shopping, recreation, schools, or water find themselves potential candidates for conversion to housing, especially in areas in which there is a scarcity of existing housing.

As is the case with most housing decisions, individual taste and preferences play a large role. The individualistic and idiosyncratic nature of older buildings holds great appeal to many buyers. For example, older buildings often have higher ceilings and more window space than is found in newer buildings. Additionally, the quality and durability of construction can be of a higher caliber in older buildings than in contemporary buildings.

The economic and financing aspects of building anew or converting are important factors. Generally speaking, it is less expensive to convert an existing building to housing than to build an entirely new structure. Building services and infrastructures, such as water, electricity, and sewage, usually exist and do not have to be newly constructed. Additionally, conversion of an existing building for use as housing can often be completed in less time than it takes to complete a new construction project.

Controlled and/or regulated growth is a factor that can determine the feasibility of converting old buildings to residential use. In areas of the country with moratoria on growth, the reuse of existing buildings has become nearly a necessity. Slow-growth moratoria generally attempt to control new hook-ups of utilities as a method of controlling construction. However, because existing buildings already have sewer, water, and electrical and/or gas hook-ups in place, they generally are not subject to the limits placed on new construction under growth moratoria.

Historic preservation and other zoning regulations are also important factors in creating a demand for new housing in old buildings. Some historic preservation ordinances prohibit the demolition of existing buildings and, in areas of the country with a demand for increased housing, the reuse of old buildings is sometimes the only alternative that can generate additional units of housing.

Some types of buildings can be more easily converted to modern residential units than others. For example, factory buildings are good candidates for a number of reasons. The general lack of permanent interior partitions in factory buildings allows easy manipulation of interior spaces without extensive demolition and construction; this makes installation of services such as plumbing and electricity easier and less expensive. Additionally, most factory buildings have large expanses of windows that make them extremely desirable as candidates for residential use. Open spaces and numerous, large windows led to the conversion in 1973 of the first mill-to-residential project in Boston. The Piano Craft Guild Housing for Artists paved the way for many factory conversion projects.

Older school buildings (such as the Carbery School Building in Washington, D.C. shown here) are good candidates for conversion to housing. Like factories, they usually have many large windows and were designed with excellent circulation patterns.

Other building types such as large single-family houses require more work for conversion to multifamily residential use. The provision of upgraded services, such as water and electricity, necessitates careful planning.

Although it is often cheaper to renovate an existing building than to construct a new residential unit, there is, without a doubt, a greater challenge in making

Completed in 1973, the conversion of the Chickering Piano Factory into the Piano Craft Guild in Boston, Massachusetts, was one of the first adaptive reuse projects in the country to convert abandoned mill buildings into housing. Since that time, the assets of mill buildings that lend themselves to ready conversion to housing have been widely recognized. Photographic credit: Greg Heins.

The Carbery School on Capitol Hill in Washington, D.C. has been converted to apartments. The location is extremely convenient for people who work in the surrounding area. Photographic credit: Peter H. Smeallie.

a successful transformation of an old building into modern, convenient housing than in new construction. The interiors of existing buildings are subject to the greatest amount of change in a residential conversion; alterations of the exteriors of such buildings are often relatively minor and intended to maintain the architectural character of the existing structure.

Interior design and space planning require the most attention to produce attractive and livable space. The interior space of an old building generally has to be reconfigured so that electrical capacity can be upgraded, modern plumbing and HVAC systems can be installed, and other requirements can be fulfilled.

The interior arrangement of dwelling units in an old building will be controlled by a number of factors. First, the existing structural system is the major determinant in the overall outline of the placement of units. Although an existing structural system can be modified, the costs of such modification have to be balanced against the additional space that may be gained as a result of the elimination of overly large and/or bulky structural elements.

Second, required building and life safety (fire) codes dictate, to a certain extent, the choice of materials and the configuration of units. Adequate means of egress and exit must be provided.

Third, the design of individual units should strive to take advantage of any visually interesting features that are present. For example, large windows can become the focal point of room arrangements. Views should be considered in determining the interior layout of a building being converted to residential use. Similarly, features such as existing fireplaces and wall panelling can focus the layout of individual units.

Modern plumbing and HVAC services can present challenges in residential conversion projects. Generally, new systems need to be installed; such systems must be provided to each individual dwelling unit in the building, and a level of individual control of services, such as heat and air conditioning, should be available in each unit.

Automobile parking is also an important consideration. Most building codes mandate that a certain percentage of parking spaces be available for residential development, depending on the number of dwelling units in the building. If the required amount of parking is not available immediately adjacent to the residential building, such space will usually have to be created. For example, parking is usually inadequate when a large home, such as a mansion, is converted to apartments or condominiums. A portion of the grounds could be used as the parking area to meet the expanded use of the property. In other instances, such as inner city areas, land in the vicinity of the converted building may have to be acquired and dedicated to parking. In addition to requirements for parking, the availability of parking is an important amenity that can be a strong feature for prospective tenants of the project.

The treatment of the landscape surrounding an old building converted to housing is an issue that frequently arises. In many cases, old buildings that are converted to residential use are surrounded by open space that creates opportunities for amenities. Plantings throughout the grounds surrounding an existing building offer the opportunity to create points of visual interest as the seasons change. Plantings can also be used to develop areas for contemplation and solitude. Opportunities to create vistas and overlooks should be exploited. Open space can also be converted for recreational uses such as baseball fields, tennis courts, and hiking or jogging paths that enhance the appeal of a residential use of an old building.

1840 Mill Building Converted to Apartments for the Elderly

In Blackstone Falls, just outside of Providence, Rhode Island, an 1840 mill building was rehabilitated and combined with new construction to create a complex of 133 units of elderly housing. The complex consists of the original mill building, which was substantially rehabilitated, and two new wings. One wing, across the mill race, was built over an existing rubble foundation of the original boiler room that powered the mill. The other wing is entirely new construction and is attached to the existing historic mill building. The complex includes parking for 48 automobiles.

The brick facades of the new wings repeat the prevailing visual element of the historic mill building. The developers of the site made use of several prominent features. The visually striking mill building tower serves as the main entrance to the complex, and a boiler room was converted into a two-story space that is used as a community room. The waterway, which runs through the property and originally powered the mill complex, is spanned by several bridges that connect the three wings of the complex. One especially noteworthy feature of this development is the installation of new water turbines to take advantage of the water power of the Blackstone River flowing through the property. The electricity is used throughout the complex, and the excess is sold to the local utility company.

An 1840 mill building just outside of Providence, Rhode Island, has been converted and combined with new construction into 133 units of elderly housing. The redevelopment plan included construction of a new wing, a new building over an existing foundation, and connections between the project elements over the historic Blackstone River. Photographic credit: Bruner/Cott & Associates, Inc.

CREDITS
NAME & LOCATION: Blackstone Falls, Central Falls, Rhode Island
ARCHITECT: Bruner/Cott & Associates, Inc., Cambridge, Massachusetts
DEVELOPER: Blackstone Falls Associates, Cambridge, Massachusetts

The Crown & Eagle Mills in Uxbridge, Massachusetts, built ca. 1825–1827, was one of the earliest textile mills in the nation. The mill continued in operation for a century, closing in 1926. The picturesque siting of the mill complex was one of the principal inducements to convert the mill into an elderly housing complex, despite a devastating fire in the mid-1970s. In the redevelopment, fragments of the original buildings were reused, and the historic silhouette was reproduced. Photographic credit: Nick Wheeler.

CREDITS
NAME & LOCATION: Crown and Eagle Apartments, Uxbridge, Massachusetts
ARCHITECT: Bruner/Cott & Associates, Inc., Cambridge, Massachusetts
DEVELOPER: Greater Boston Community Development, Boston, Massachusetts

Cotton Mill Becomes Apartment Complex

The Crown and Eagle Mills in Uxbridge, Massachusetts was one of the most picturesque mill complexes in New England. Built in 1825–1827, the mill was one of the earliest textile mills erected in the country. It operated for nearly a century until 1926. In 1975 a major fire virtually destroyed the complex. A survey indicated that there was a substantial need for elderly housing in the area. Despite the fire devastation, the amenities of the site— open space, river, and canals—provided sufficient attraction to undertake a major reconstruction project to turn the ruins of the old mill complex into a residential apartment project. The fragments of the old mill that could be reused were incorporated into the new structure, which reproduced the historic silhouette of the mill buildings. The focal point of the development remained the power canals and the river.

Extensive landscaping, including plantings along the river's edge, was combined with a pedestrian bridge over the canal and a water garden created from the remains of the former mill wheelhouse. The apartment complex, completed in 1984, contains 62 units and a parking area for 43 cars.

Victorian Warehouse Renovated for Shops and Apartments

Two late nineteenth-century warehouse structures in the Strand Historic District in Galveston, Texas have been remodeled into a complex of four retail stores and eight apartments. The buildings had been entirely stripped of all orna-

The Springer Building in the Strand Historic District of Galveston, Texas, was remodeled out of two former nineteenth-century warehouses. All ornamentation had been stripped from the buildings in the 1930s and a new trompe l'oeil facade was created in 1978. Photographic credit: Taft Associates.

CREDITS
NAME & LOCATION: Springer Building, Galveston, Texas
ARCHITECT: Taft Associates, Houston, Texas

mentation in the 1930s. A painted trompe l'oeil facade was created by muralist Richard Haas in 1978. In the remodeling work, all interior partitions were removed and replaced. The apartments are organized around the mechanical core that serves the bathroom and kitchen. A skylit atrium links the two buildings and provides for vertical circulation between the floors as well as a common garden room. High ceiling heights on the second level allowed the installation of mezzanines. Careful attention was paid to the interior detailing and painted stencilling in the common areas of the buildings.

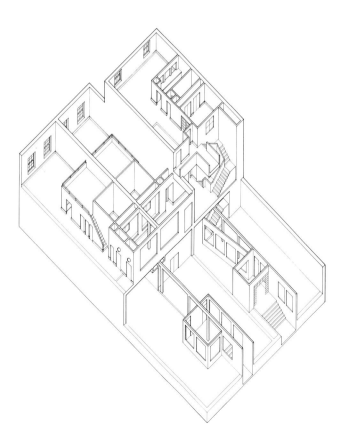

The buildings have been remodeled into shops and apartments. A central skylight atrium provides the connection between the two buildings, and high ceiling heights allows a second level in the apartments. Drawing credit: Taft Associates.

43

Waterfront Wharf Building into Urban Apartment Complex

In the nineteenth century when it was built, the Mercantile Building was an important part of the bustling harbor of Boston. Sailing ships could tie up at the building's dock to load and unload goods. As Boston grew around the building and the method of transportation for the shipment of goods changed from ships to trains and then to trucks, the Mercantile Building ceased to be important as part of the port of Boston. Eventually, the building found itself several blocks inland from the actual Boston waterfront.

In 1976 the Mercantile Building was transformed into an apartment and retail complex. Its location in the heart of Boston's downtown business district makes the building extraordinarily convenient for residents who work nearby. The numerous windows of the original structure provide not only daylight but

The Mercantile Wharf building in Boston, Massachusetts was once directly on Boston's waterfront. Today, it is several blocks away from the actual waterfront and has been converted into a retail and apartment complex. Photographic credit: Steve Rosenthal.

CREDITS
NAME & LOCATION: Mercantile Wharf Building, Boston, Massachusetts
ARCHITECT: John Sharratt Associates, Inc., Boston, Massachusetts
OWNER: Mercantile Associates, Boston, Massachusetts

The apartments include industrial structural elements of the original building.
Photographic credit: Steve Rosenthal.

also afford residents a view of Boston harbor. Skylights cut into the roof of the building provide additional daylight to the residents on the top floor.

A central atrium was carved out of the interior of the building, and the building's interior circulation system including the elevators is located off the atrium. Landscaping of the immediately adjacent areas provides an attractive park for recreational activities.

Nineteenth-Century Mansion into Apartments

A mid-nineteenth-century mansion that had once been Albert Einstein's first home in the United States has been converted into five apartments. The reuse of the building involves the sensitive reconfiguration of interior partitions in the building to create the five apartments, four of which are duplexes with

In Princeton, New Jersey, a nineteenth-century mansion that is owned by the Princeton Theological Seminary has been converted into five apartments. The grounds have also been restored and are an important part of the overall project. Photographic credit: Otto Baitz.

CREDITS
NAME & LOCATION: 2 Library Place, Princeton, New Jersey
ARCHITECT: Short and Ford Architects, Princeton, New Jersey
DEVELOPER: Princeton Theological Seminary, Princeton, New Jersey

fireplaces. Considerable structural work was also needed to complete the conversion. The grounds of the mansion are carefully landscaped and continue to be an important element in the overall development.

Trolley Barn into Large Apartment Complex

The East Capitol Street Car Barn in Washington, D.C. is a massive building that was used to store and service trolleys when they were operating throughout the city. The building, which occupies an entire city block within sight of the U.S. Capitol, was built in 1896 as a terminus of the Washington trolley system. The front of the building on East Capitol Street and the large central tower have been converted into 52 one- and two-bedroom apartments. The rear facade is new and contains openings for light and ventilation into the living spaces. It is scaled to reflect the rhythm on the major street facade. The rest of the complex includes 144 new townhouses built within the original exterior walls surrounding the train sheds. Parking is also included within the project's walls. Martin & Jones of Washington, D.C., the architects for the project, received an Award for Excellence in Design for this complex from the American Institute of Architects.

The East Capitol Street Car Barn in Washington, D.C. was built as a terminus of the city's trolley system in 1896. Photographic credit: Maxwell Mackenzie.

CREDITS
NAME & LOCATION: East Capitol Car Barn, Washington, D.C.
ARCHITECT: Martin & Jones Architects, Washington, D.C.
DEVELOPER: Richmarr Construction Co., Washington, D.C.

The main section of the building fronting on East Capitol Street, N.E., within site of the U.S. Capitol, has been turned into 52 apartments. The street facade has been preserved while the rear facade is completely new to allow for openings into the apartments. Drawing credit: Martin & Jones, Architects.

Side Elevation

Section

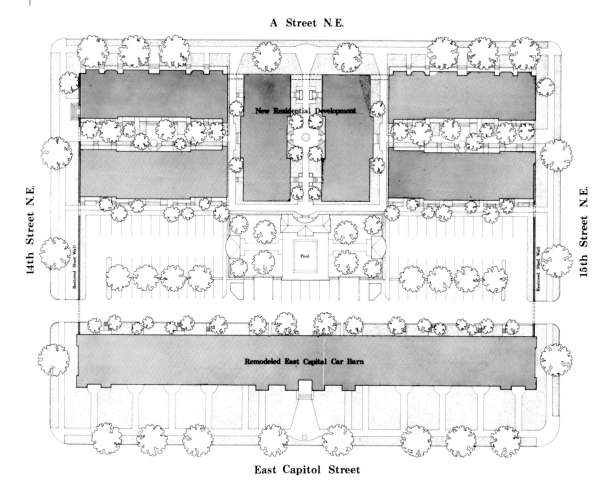

The site occupies an entire city block and includes not only the apartments but 144 new townhouses within the walls of the original train sheds. Parking is included in the interior of the site. Drawing credit: Martin & Jones, Architects.

Old Church into Residential Units

On Capitol Hill in Washington, D.C. a number of abandoned schools and churches have been converted for residential use. Because, unlike so many other American cities, Washington had no industrial base, opportunities for the conversion of abandoned factories and warehouses do not exist. Instead, in the historic districts of Washington, small and medium-size buildings are being converted to residential uses.

The Faith Baptist Church, built in 1891, stands only a few blocks from the U.S. Capitol. As the population of Capitol Hill changed, the church's congregation moved on. There remained a historic romanesque, twin-turreted, brick church building. The church has been converted into a residential building with 23 units. Because of the shape of the building, the units are quite individualistic in layout. Parking for the residents was required to be on the site. This was achieved by putting parking inside the building.

The entrance to the garage was created by greatly enlarging a side door beneath a stained glass window of the former church. Repairs to the exterior of the building were carried out with similar materials, except on the roof where synthetic tiles were used to replace damaged polychrome slate tiles on the original roof.

The Faith Baptist Church in Washington, D.C. was built in 1891. Today, it has been turned into 23 individualistic apartments, with parking, which is located on the lower level of the structure and is reached through an entryway cut into the wall of the former church beneath a large stained glass window.
Photographic credit: Peter H. Smith.

CREDITS
NAME & LOCATION: Faith Baptist Church, Washington, D.C.
ARCHITECT: Robert Schwartz, Washington, D.C.

Old City Hall Converted into Apartments

In Harrisburg, Pennsylvania the former City Hall has been converted into an apartment complex. The building, originally built as a vocational/technical high school in 1905, became City Hall in 1927. After the municipal government moved out, a market survey determined that the building could best be converted to a residential building of one-bedroom units. The building's 16-foot ceiling heights led to an approach that developed a loft level to serve as the bedroom in each of the units. The bedrooms overlook a full height living area. The apartment units were standardized as much as possible, and most units have identical floor plans.

Mechanical equipment is located on the loft level over the corridors. The high ceilings in the corridors are broken up by introducing lower ceiling heights at apartment entryways to house the mechanical equipment. This approach also has the added advantage of allowing for different treatments at the apartment entrances.

Harrisburg, Pennsylvania's old city hall was converted into an apartment complex. The one-block site permitted the development of a landscaped parking area for the complex, including a handicapped access ramp into the building. Drawing credit: The Rothschild Company/ Architects.

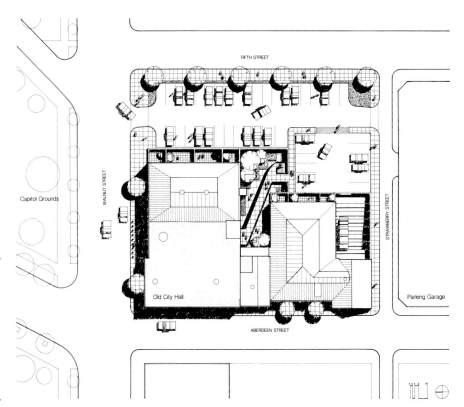

CREDITS
NAME & LOCATION: Harrisburg Old City Hall, Harrisburg, Pennsylvania
ARCHITECT: Elliot J. Rothschild, AIA, The Rothschild Company/ Architects, Philadelphia, Pennsylvania
DEVELOPER: Historic Landmarks for Living, Inc., Philadelphia, Pennsylvania

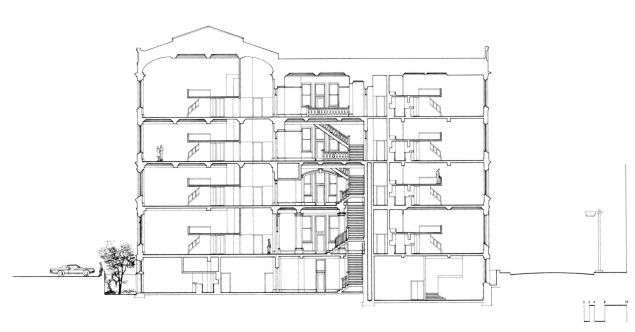

The 16-foot ceiling heights in the building allowed the development of a loft bedroom level in many of the apartment units. Careful planning permitted the retention of the central grand staircase as an important interior feature. A restaurant was developed in the basement level of the building. Drawing credit: The Rothschild Company/Architects.

Important interior features, including the grand stair hall, were restored; the Mayor's office serves as the apartment building manager's office. A restaurant is located in the basement of the building, and a landscaped parking lot for 46 automobiles is located on site.

Multibuilding Wire Mill Complex to Apartments

The Alfred F. Moore Factory complex, built during the nineteenth century, occupies an entire city block in Philadelphia about 25 feet from the Benjamin Franklin Bridge that links the city with New Jersey. The large complex of heavy timber and brick construction includes 100,000 square feet of space on six different levels, including one below grade. It is part of the Old City Historic District of Philadelphia. The goal of the project's developer was to reuse the large complex as studio and one-bedroom apartments while preserving the wood industrial elements of the buildings.

The Wireworks, an apartment complex, was created out of a former factory building in Philadelphia, Pennsylvania. The factory occupied an entire city block and included 100,000 square feet of space on six levels. A heavy wood trellis at the entrance to the development echoes the heavy timber construction of the industrial plant. Photographic credit: Elliot Kaufman.

CREDITS
NAME & LOCATION: *The Wireworks, Philadelphia, Pennsylvania*
ARCHITECT: *Elliot J. Rothschild, AIA, The Rothschild Company/ Architects, Philadelphia, Pennsylvania*
DEVELOPER: *Historic Landmarks for Living, Inc., Philadelphia, Pennsylvania*

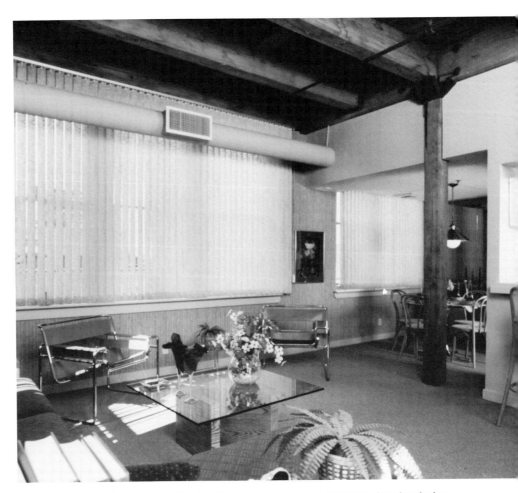

The structural wood elements of the building were incorporated into the interior design of the apartments and were a significant factor in determining unit layouts. Ductwork for the HVAC system was exposed as part of the overall interior design scheme. Photographic credit: Elliot Kaufman.

The site presented a number of challenges. Poor circulation throughout the site was solved by developing a richly landscaped walkway. The entrance to the complex is through a heavy timber pedestrian bridge that passes over the landscaped courtyard. A double-loaded corridor system connects all parts of the complex and the elevators. In addition, three fireproof stair towers serve the complex. Much of the original wood framing system of the buildings has been retained, as well as the enormous windows that offer spectacular views of the Benjamin Franklin Bridge.

The decision to retain the wood columns was the major factor influencing the layout of the individual units. Because so much of the wood framing was retained, adequate soundproofing was required. This was achieved by pouring a 3/4-inch concrete slab directly on top of the 3-inch wood flooring and then laying carpeting over the surface. Additionally, exposing the wood framing members meant that the heating and air-conditioning ducts would have to be exposed. Specially designed duct work was used and placed so that it suggested interior room arrangements. Mechanical equipment for each unit was placed above the apartment entrance foyers, allowing an increase in the usable square footage of each unit.

A former horse barn has been converted into a weekend residence. The center of the U-shaped building is the main living area; one wing contains the kitchen and bath area and the other serves as a special purpose room.

CREDITS
NAME & LOCATION: Weekend Residence, Oyster Bay Cove, New York
ARCHITECT: Peter Bentel, Bentel & Bentel Architects, Locust Valley, New York

Horse Barn to Weekend House

A large and spacious horse barn on a Long Island estate has been converted into a weekend house. The center of the U-shaped building is the central living area with one of the wings serving as a special purpose room and the other as a kitchen and bath area. Access to the main bedroom, located in a loft in one of the wings, is by a circular stair that has been installed in the former silo. Careful landscaping of the grounds of the residence enhances its country atmosphere.

Warehouse to Luxury Apartments

In Pittsburgh, Pennsylvania a former hardware warehouse has been converted to luxury apartments. Built in 1903, the building is a four-story brick warehouse in a residential neighborhood within walking distance of the University of Pittsburgh and Carnegie-Mellon University. A central organizing feature of the new apartment complex is a rectangular courtyard that was cut into the middle of the square building. The courtyard allowed the creation of interior apartments and provides an outdoor space for residents.

Seventeen-foot ceiling heights on the second and fourth floors of the building allow for lofts that overlook a full-height living area. The entry to the building includes a landscaped walkway that leads through a large lobby and through the building to the interior courtyard. Parking is located adjacent to the north side of the building.

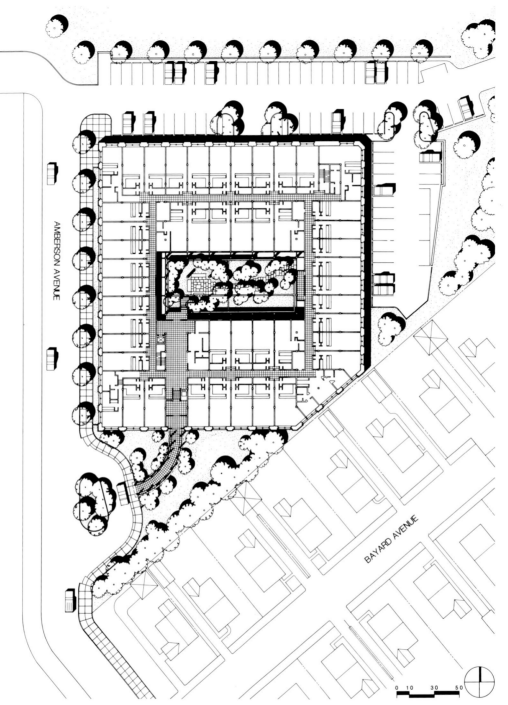

In Pittsburgh, Pennsylvania, a 1903 hardware warehouse has been converted into a luxury apartment complex. Located near the city's universities, the Shadyside Commons apartment complex is organized around a central courtyard in the middle of the building. Parking for the residents is located around the perimeter of the building. Drawing credit: The Rothschild Company/Architects.

CREDITS
NAME & LOCATION: Shadyside Commons, Pittsburgh, Pennsylvania
ARCHITECT: Elliot J. Rothschild, AIA, The Rothschild Company/Architects, Philadelphia, Pennsylvania
DEVELOPER: Historic Landmarks for Living, Inc., Philadelphia, Pennsylvania

The landscaped courtyard in the center of the building was created by cutting into the middle of the square structure. The courtyard provides both outdoor space for residents as well as light for apartments on the interior. Photographic credit: James B. Abbott.

Hospital to Condominiums

St. Joseph's Hospital in San Francisco was built in 1926 in the Spanish Revival style and consisted of three buildings: the hospital itself, a convent, and a chapel. Two of the buildings—the hospital and the convent—have been converted to 136 condominium units.

San Francisco's strict environmental laws and regulations and an active citizen's association led to extensive negotiations before construction could begin. Originally, the developer proposed that new construction be added; this was required to be scaled back so that only the existing buildings were included as part of the plan.

The building also had to be reinforced to meet California's seismic code. The hospital and convent interiors were completely gutted. Because the hospital building is only 38 feet wide, about half the width of conventional buildings, the designers devised 29 separate apartment models that are quite long with numerous windows. The project saved the original windows and the entire exterior of the buildings. The chapel serves as a community center; the interior domed roof, murals, and stained glass windows were retained. Parking for the project was created by excavating under the central plaza of the hospital building.

Historic Warehouse Complex to Retail Stores and Luxury Apartments

Three textile warehouses (two built in 1878, the other in 1906) in the Warehouse Historic District of New Orleans have been converted into 101 apartments and commercial space. A central courtyard was created by cutting through the roofs and each of the five floors of the warehouses. The concrete beams and columns define the interior arrangements, including the apartments' location and the definition of spatial functions within each unit.

St. Joseph's Hospital in San Francisco, California, built in 1926, has been converted into the Park Hill condominiums. The narrow width of the original building resulted in a wide range of different configurations for the condominium units. Photographic credit: Douglas Symes.

CREDITS
NAME & LOCATION: Park Hill, San Francisco, California
ARCHITECT: Kaplan/McLaughlin/ Diaz, San Francisco, California
DEVELOPER: The Aspen Group, San Francisco, California

In New Orleans, Louisiana, three warehouses dating from the latter part of the nineteenth century and the early part of the twentieth have been converted into an apartment complex. The former loading docks for the warehouses are now the entrance into the complex. Photographic credit: Eskew Vogt Salvato & Filson.

CREDITS
NAME & LOCATION: Julia Place, New Orleans, Louisiana
ARCHITECT: Eskew Vogt Salvato & Filson Architects, New Orleans, Louisiana
DEVELOPER: Henry Lambert, Arthur Davis and Carey Bond, New Orleans, Louisiana

Julia Place's central courtyard was created by cutting through the roof and each of the five floors of the buildings. The concrete beams and columns define the interior spatial arrangements. Photographic credit: Eskew Vogt Salvato & Filson.

Mechanical equipment for the apartments is located in the hallways above dropped ceilings. Sixteen-foot high ceilings on the top floor allowed the creation of two level apartments with magnificent views of the city. The former loading docks of the buildings were adapted as the entryways. Most of the window frames had deteriorated, and replacements were created using the original drawings.

Bank Building to Apartments for the Elderly

The Riggs National Bank Building, located in the 14th Street Historic District of Washington, D.C., was extensively renovated for apartment and retail use. The original structure consisted of four separate reinforced concrete structures, each three stories, that extended the length of an entire city block. To design a building of residential proportions, a courtyard was created by partially demolishing a portion of the rear of the structure. The courtyard also serves as the entry for the building.

In Washington, D.C. a bank building on 14th Street, N.W., was extensively renovated for apartment and retail use while continuing to function as a bank. Photographic credit: William T. Smith.

CREDITS
NAME & LOCATION: Park Road Apartments, Washington, D.C.
ARCHITECT: Boston Architectural Team, Inc., Chelsea, Massachusetts
DEVELOPER: Winn Development, Boston, Massachusetts

A courtyard for the apartments was created by demolishing a portion of the rear of the bank building. Two additional floors were added to the original height of the structure.

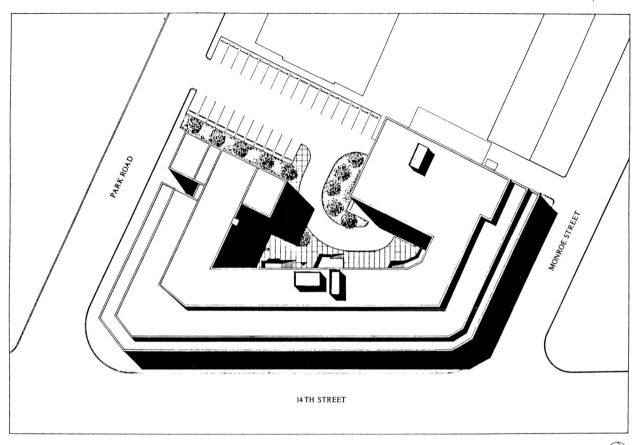

Park Road Apartments · SITE PLAN ·  0⌐⌐⌐⌐⌐⌐40 ft

The complex is U-shaped and includes parking as well as a circular entry drive. The project contains 150 apartments and 30,000 square feet of retail space. Drawing credit: Boston Architectural Team, Inc.

Two stories were added onto the original structure to create a complex of 150 one- and two-bedroom apartments. In addition, 30,000 square feet of retail space, including the bank, are located on the street level. A synthetic stucco material was used on the exterior of the new floors to retain the historic appearance of the original building's facade.

Ornamental plaster work on the interiors of the first floor retail stores was saved. To preserve this ornamentation and still allow the installation of new electric and plumbing systems, including a fire sprinkler system, a false floor was created as part of the new construction on the second floor. Throughout the construction of the project, the existing retail stores and the bank continued to operate. A circular entry drive and parking are located in the courtyard in the rear of the building.

Power Plant to Housing

A power plant, built overlooking Boston harbor by the Massachusetts Bay Transit Authority, was in operation until 1972. It has been renovated into 192 units of low-income housing. The original building contained no floors and had brick walls 3 feet thick, as well as an extensive interior steel structural system. To provide light to the interior apartments, a large atrium was created

A former power plant for the Massachusetts Bay Transit Authority in Boston, Massachusetts has been converted into the San Marco/Lincoln Wharf apartment complex. Photographic credit: Bruce T. Martin.

CREDITS
NAME & LOCATION: *San Marco/Lincoln Wharf, Boston, Massachusetts*
ARCHITECT: *Boston Architectural Team, Inc., Chelsea, Massachusetts*
DEVELOPER: *San Marco Housing Corporation, Boston, Massachusetts*

The power plant building had plain brick walls. In order to convert the building to apartments, 300 windows were punched through the walls to provide light for the apartments.

Inside the building a large atrium was created to provide light to the interior of the apartments and to create a circulation system. The interior steel structural system was retained and used to support the skylight. Photographic credit: Bruce T. Martin.

along the width of the building. Corridors overlooking the atrium were built. The interior steel structural system was retained and used to support a skylight over the atrium. The steelwork was covered with gypsum wallboard as a fireproofing measure.

The original power plant building had plain brick walls with no fenestration. Three hundred windows had to be punched through the walls for the apartments. The public has access to the waterfront via the atrium. Three glass-enclosed elevators were added at one end of the building.

Historic High School Buildings Become Apartment Complex

In Mechanicsburg, Pennsylvania a high school complex that is listed on the National Register of Historic Places has been transformed into a 60-apartment unit complex. The site includes two buildings: a two-story 1892 Romanesque

In Mechanicsburg, Pennsylvania, two former school buildings—an 1892 Romanesque red brick building, pictured here, and a 1929 Gothic Revival building—were combined with new construction to create the School House, a 60 apartment unit complex. Photographic credit: The Rothschild Company/Architects.

CREDITS
NAME & LOCATION: The School House, Mechanicsburg, Pennsylvania
ARCHITECT: Michael Hauptman, The Rothschild Company/Architects, Philadelphia, Pennsylvania
DEVELOPER: Historic Landmarks for Living, Inc., Philadelphia, Pennsylvania

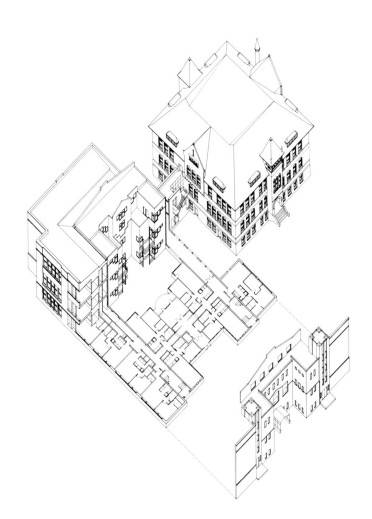

New apartment units were created by filling in a central courtyard; the two buildings were combined with a connecting walkway. Drawing credit: The Rothschild Company/Architects.

red brick building and a three-story 1929 Gothic Revival yellow brick building with decorative brownstone.

The conversion work on the 1892 structure did not require altering the original plan of the building. The central hall plan was preserved as well as much of the original wainscoting and trim. The original windows of the building were retained and restored. Code variances were obtained to permit keeping the original doors and stairs.

Work on the 1929 building was more extensive. The interior hallways were narrowed to create a more residential scale. This permitted the development of entry alcoves and ancillary spaces. The building's auditorium was demolished to construct 18 apartment units that surround a central courtyard on three levels.

A small one-story addition to the 1892 building was demolished to construct an elevator, mailroom, and lobby for the complex. Several other small buildings on the site were also demolished for parking and landscaping.

5

Conversion to Offices

Office space can be found in all kinds of buildings—warehouses, factories, even old laundries. Offices created from old space are often preferred to routine and repetitive modern office buildings. Many businesses and professional firms feel strongly that old spaces are better for their employees and, thus, better for their business.

Regardless of the setting or historical context, office space needs to be adaptable as businesses expand and contract. Facility management literature reports record "churn" rates—the turnover of office employees that has physical and spatial implications. The need for flexibility is found in systems furniture, a common element in many landscaped offices today. Accompanying the need for flexibility are the needs of the electronically enhanced office, the "smart office."

The office landscape of the 1980s is considerably different than that of a decade ago and will most likely be considerably different a decade from now. The electronic office is a maze of plugged-in technologies—duplicating machines, fax machines, computers, and other automated systems. Simply accommodating the wiring necessary to link computers to one another and to the outside world may require a new floor level to put the cabling between the original and the new floor. Often designers will drop a false ceiling to conceal wiring.

There are design challenges in these strategies. For example, decorative elements on the floor or ceiling should be considered before a false floor or ceiling is constructed. The Longworth building in Washington, D.C., which houses Congressional offices, underwent considerable changes in an upgrading project for computers. Because the floors of the building are concrete and construction of a false floor would disrupt the operations of Congress, and because the ceilings are relatively high, cabling for the computers has been installed in overhead channels suspended from the ceiling.

When older buildings are adapted for office space, the availability and distribution of natural lighting from windows are high-priority items. Therefore, designers should consider the location of windows as well as the distribution

Channels for computer cables on the ceiling of the Longworth House Office Building. Photographic credit: Peter H. Smeallie.

patterns of natural light when determining the location of partitions or office walls. In some cases, additional window openings may need to be created. Care should be taken to ensure that important design elements of the original structure are not destroyed or significantly altered.

As economic conditions and the technology of offices change, older office spaces will require upgrading. In most cases where the interior is renovated, the tenants move out, the building is refurbished, and new tenants are sought. However, in rare examples, major conversion and upgrading of the interior of a building take place with the tenants remaining in the building.

Such was the case with the National Press Building in Washington, D.C. The National Press Building, originally designed as a Beaux-Arts-style building located between the Capitol and the White House, houses a large number of news organizations that report on activities in Washington. A major rehabilitation of the building was undertaken in the early 1980s to upgrade the interior spaces and to bring in the latest telecommunication technologies. In addition to the interior upgrading, which included the creation of a multistory atrium linking the building with an adjacent shopping complex, the entire facade of the structure, which fronts on two streets, was replaced.

All the work was carried out while the tenants remained in the building. To accommodate their work, tenants were shifted to other office space within the building, while work was undertaken on their suite. One project manager described it as a three-dimensional game of checkers. Keeping the construction on schedule was not easy, and the construction noise, dust, and dirt played havoc with many of the tenants. Many could not tolerate the disruptions and left during the course of construction. Major office improvement projects are complex undertakings with existing tenants in place.

In reusing existing buildings for new office space, parking for prospective office tenants is a major consideration. Most new office space requires parking; indeed, most zoning codes for any type of building require a specified number of parking spaces depending on the size of the development. Finding the space for automobile parking can be difficult and expensive, and can endanger the historical integrity of many projects, if not handled correctly.

In developments that combine a substantial amount of new construction,

The National Press Building in Washington, D.C. underwent a major rehabilitation including a new facade while the tenants remained in the building. Photographic credit: Peter H. Smith.

As part of the overall program, an interior atrium was created to link the building with an adjacent retail shopping complex. Photographic credit: Peter H. Smith.

as with the rehabilitation of an existing building, parking can often be located in the new portion of the building. Generally, in such cases, parking can be constructed below grade. In other cases, parking must be sought on the site of the project or nearby. For example, the site surrounding an existing building could be graded and dedicated to parking or land in the immediate vicinity could be acquired and developed as parking for tenants of the building. Whatever the case, parking is a necessary amenity for any new office development.

Adequate delivery areas are needed in office conversions. Ideally, a loading dock should be located to the rear of the building and allow delivery vehicles to pull directly up to the loading dock. Older buildings are often not designed to accommodate modern delivery techniques; supplies coming in and trash going out share the same entryway used by the occupants. Facilities that permit some other method of delivery should be sought before delivery through the main entrance is adopted.

Heating and cooling of office buildings have special requirements. In buildings that are wholly occupied by offices, heating and cooling are often provided only during normal working hours. At other times of the day or over the weekend, building HVAC systems are generally not operated except to maintain a minimum temperature level to support the building's mechanical systems.

Many new buildings are essentially sealed structures, having no operable windows. This means that the HVAC system is operated on the assumption that the building users do not have control over introducing fresh air—hot or cold—into their offices. In some buildings the electrical lighting is an integral part of the heating system of the building that relies on the heat generated by the electrical lights to provide a portion of the building's heating load. An HVAC system that relies on closed windows in a rehabilitated office building can create anomalies. For example, the Old Post Office in Washington, D.C., built in 1899, has numerous windows on all eight of its floors. When the building was rehabilitated for new offices in the early 1980s, a central HVAC system was installed. Clear plexiglass panels were screwed to the inside window frames throughout the building to create the proper interior climate with this closed HVAC system. Although the outward appearance of the building has not changed, office tenants can no longer make use of the windows as they were intended.

Adapting existing buildings to modern office needs creates challenges in complying with building and fire codes. Large, open stairways are often present in many older multistory buildings and in many residences. Ceremonial stairways, built before the invention of the elevator or escalator, often are the central focal point of a historic building's interior. They are often at odds with fire codes because they can act as giant flues in the event of fire, spreading the fire rapidly throughout the building. In many rehabilitation projects open stairways are eliminated, and the space they occupied becomes additional office space. Another common solution is to enclose completely the stairway and install fire doors on each floor.

In buildings in which the stairway is an integral feature of the interior design, it is possible to enclose the stairwell in glass, meeting the fire code while maintaining the visual importance of the stairway. Such is the case in a former nineteenth-century residential rowhouse converted into offices in Washington, D.C. A stairway connects all four floors of the building. Today, it is completely enclosed in glass and continues to provide a central means of circulation throughout the offices, while at the same time meeting current city fire codes.

The lobby of an office building is the first interior space encountered by workers and visitors. As such, it is a crucial element in setting the tone for

The art moderne-style bus station in downtown Washington, D.C. will become part of a large new office complex and serve as the entrance and lobby area for the development scheduled for completion in 1991. Drawing credit: Keyes Condon Florance Architects.

CREDITS
NAME & LOCATION: 1100 New York Avenue, Washington, D.C.
ARCHITECT: Keyes Condon Florance Architects, Washington, D.C.
OWNER: Manufacturers Life Real Estate

the building and it generally has greater detailing than is found on other floors. In addition, the lobby serves several critical functions. It is an orientation point to provide information on the tenants and a sense of direction. It serves as a meeting place for workers and others. The lobby is also of prime importance for building security and can serve as a check point to monitor traffic into and out of the building.

The lobby must be easily recognized. In some large projects, especially those that combine more than one building, finding the lobby is not always an easy task. In some multiuse projects that combine retailing activities with office space, the lobby area blends into the background and appears to be just another attraction. Lobby space should be clearly segregated from other uses in a building, but should not be hidden.

One unusual approach to creating lobby space combines new and old buildings in Washington, D.C. There, after a lengthy preservation battle, the downtown 1940s Art Moderne-style Greyhound bus terminal will be restored and become the lobby area of a $130 million new office tower.

Warehouse to Prime Retail and Office Space

Twenty North Michigan Avenue in Chicago was originally built to house the catalogue sales operation of Montgomery Ward. It subsequently became a retail furniture store and warehouse. The building occupies an important location along Michigan Avenue, one of Chicago's busiest streets. It is built of masonry and timber, and contains approximately 200,000 gross square feet of space. In 1982 the building was rehabilitated into modern office and retail space including new plumbing, electrical, HVAC, and sprinkler systems. The elevators were remodeled as part of the renovation plan. To bring light into interior offices, a 1,500-square foot atrium was cut through the building from the roof to ground level. A series of graduated setbacks of the retail store fronts on the interior of the building was created to diminish the visual distance from the entryway to the elevator bank and to make the walk more interesting.

Twenty North Michigan Avenue in Chicago, Illinois was originally built to house the operations of Montgomery Ward. It has been remodeled as modern office and retail space. Photographic credit: Hedrick-Blessing.

CREDITS
NAME & LOCATION: Twenty North Michigan Avenue Building, Chicago, Illinois
ARCHITECT: Nagle, Hartray & Associates, Ltd., Chicago, Illinois
DEVELOPER: U.S. Equities, Inc., Chicago, Illinois

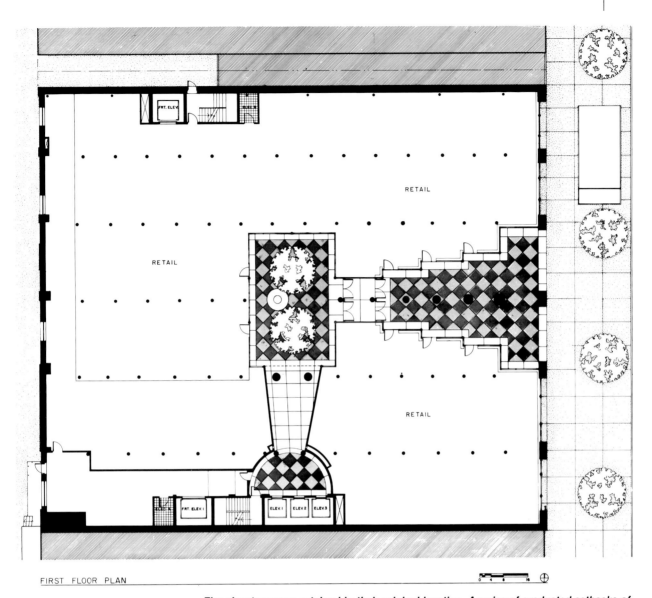

FIRST FLOOR PLAN

The elevators were retained in their original location. A series of graduated setbacks of the retail store fronts on the interior of the building diminishes the visual distance from the entrance to the elevators as well as creates an active shopping area. Photographic credit: K&S Photographics.

The base of the building was redesigned using limestone and granite, and new entries were created to encourage pedestrian traffic into the ground floor retail shops.

Municipal Building to Private Offices

116 South Michigan Avenue in Chicago was originally built in 1906 as the Chicago Municipal Building. When city offices moved elsewhere, the building was renovated for modern office use. The original terra cotta facade of the building was refurbished and the original lobby was elegantly renovated. The work on the lobby included installation of new marble, decorative plaster,

116 South Michigan Avenue in Chicago, Illinois was originally built in 1906 as the Chicago Municipal Building. The building has been remodeled into modern office space. Photographic credit: Pappageorge/Haymes Ltd.

CREDITS
NAME & LOCATION: 116 South Michigan Avenue, Chicago, Illinois
ARCHITECT: Mark Sullivan, Pappageorge/Haymes Ltd., Chicago, Illinois

The remodeling included the creation of retail space at the base of the building.
Photographic credit: Pappageorge/Haymes Ltd.

terrazzo, and bronze doors. The entryway is sympathetic to the original design of the building and creates retail space at the base of the building.

Nineteenth-Century Meeting House to Offices and Residence

In the Beacon Hill section of Boston, the nineteenth-century Charles Street Meeting House has been converted into three levels of office space for an architectural firm, a series of retail shops on the street level, and an unusual residence in the bell tower. New floors were inserted in the structure in the former sanctuary to create the office space. The lobby to the office building uses the former main entrance into the church. General circulation between the various office levels is by a series of stairs. In addition, an elevator in the lobby area provides circulation to the upper floors. A residence in the bell tower of the former church has different functions on different levels. A small elevator provides access from the street level to the upper floors of the apartment.

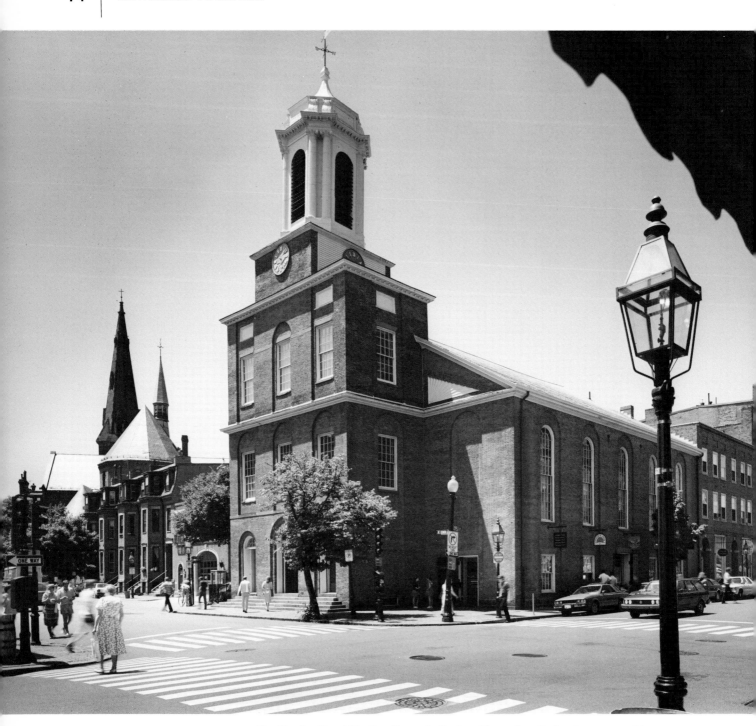

The Charles Street Meeting House in Boston, Massachusetts has been reused for offices, retail space, and an unusual residence in the bell tower. Photographic credit: Steve Rosenthal.

CREDITS
NAME & LOCATION: Charles Street Meeting House, Boston, Massachusetts
ARCHITECT: John Sharratt Associates, Inc., Boston, Massachusetts
OWNER: Charles Street Meeting House Associates, Boston, Massachusetts

New levels have been created in the former sanctuary space for the building's use as an architectural office. Photographic credit: Steve Rosenthal.

Retail space is located on the first floor of the structure fronting the street, office space is located above, and residential space has been created in the bell tower. Drawing credit: John Sharratt Associates, Inc.

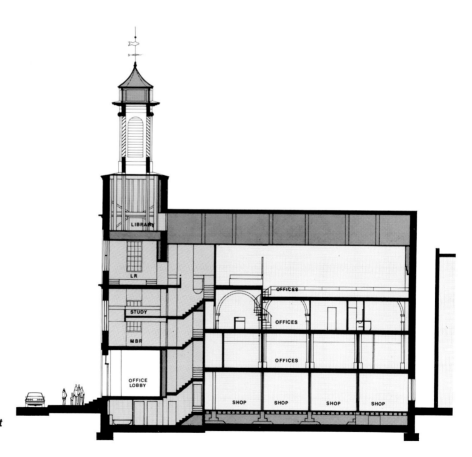

BUILDING SECTION A-A

Nineteenth-Century Commercial Block to Retail and Office Space

A nineteenth-century commercial block in Boston's Back Bay area has become the home of Burberry's, the London retailer. The building, an important part of the architectural heritage of Back Bay, had been almost completely destroyed in a major fire. The architects for the restoration of the building designed a new six-story steel frame to be constructed within the shell of the ruined walls. A new facade was designed that echoed the original building. Additional space for offices was created by adding a sixth story and an additional bay on one side of the building. The building contains slightly over 12,500 square feet of space. Burberry's occupies about half of the total space and is located on three floors plus the basement of the renovated structure. The three other floors are devoted to office space.

A nineteenth-century commercial block in the Back Bay area of Boston, Massachusetts is the home of the Boston branch of Burberry's. Before remodeling began, the building was almost destroyed by fire. The renovation involved the construction of a steel frame within the shell of the ruined walls, the development of a new facade to replace the burned area, and the addition of a sixth story for additional space. Photographic credit: Steve Rosenthal.

CREDITS
NAME & LOCATION: Burberry House, Boston, Massachusetts
ARCHITECT: Bruner/Cott & Associates, Inc., Boston, Massachusetts
DEVELOPER: Burberry's, Limited, London, England and New York, New York

New England Waterfront Structure to Office Space

The Rodman Candleworks, located in the historic waterfront district of New Bedford, Massachusetts, is an early example of New Bedford Federal-style architecture. Distinctive quoins surround the windows and doorways on the south and west facades of the building as well as delineate the corners of the building. By the late 1970s the building was derelict. Through a joint effort

The architecturally distinctive Rodman Candleworks on the waterfront in New Bedford, Massachusetts has been revitalized as an office building and includes a restaurant on one level. Photographic credit: Steve Rosenthal.

CREDITS
NAME & LOCATION: Rodman Candleworks, New Bedford, Massachusetts
ARCHITECT: Bruner/Cott & Associates, Inc., Boston, Massachusetts
DEVELOPER: Architectural Conservation Trust with Waterfront Historic Area League, New Bedford, Massachusetts

LOCATION PLAN

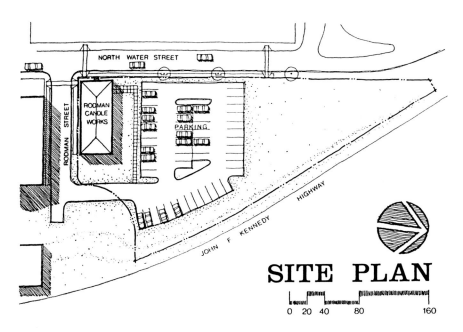

Parking to accommodate the new uses of the building is located directly behind the historic building. Drawing credit: Bruner/ Cott & Associates, Inc.

SITE PLAN

0 20 40   80   160

of the City of New Bedford, the Massachusetts Historical Commission, and the Waterfront Historic Area League of New Bedford, the building was renovated for modern office use. Two floors of the building are occupied by a bank, and offices of a law firm are located on the upper level. The lower level houses a restaurant. The original entrance of the building was maintained, and a new elevator lobby was added. Parking for all uses of the building is located adjacent to the renovated structure.

The 1890–1892 Sullivan & Adler Wainwright Building in St. Louis, Missouri, which served as the prototype for the modern skyscraper, was saved from demolition and, through an imaginative design competition, has been turned into offices for the State of Missouri government.

CREDITS
NAME & LOCATION: Wainwright State Office Building, St. Louis, Missouri
ARCHITECT OF THE WAINWRIGHT BUILDING: Louis Sullivan
ARCHITECTS OF THE RENOVATION AND ADDITION: Hastings + Chivetta and Mitchell/Giurgola
PLANNERS AND INTERIOR ARCHITECTS: Team Four, St. Louis, Missouri

Landmark Conversion to State Offices

Many older office buildings are continually refurbished to accommodate new business requirements. However, only within the last couple of decades have unused or underused buildings, many not originally designed for office space, been rehabilitated or transformed to office space. A celebrated and, in many ways, a landmark case for the preservation movement took place in the mid-1970s.

By combining old architecture with new construction, one of the most important early skyscrapers, the Wainwright Building, in St. Louis, Missouri has been resurrected as offices for various functions of the state government. The Wainwright Building, designed by Adler and Sullivan and built in 1892, was threatened with demolition in 1974. The National Trust for Historic Preservation committed itself to saving the structure and took an option to purchase the building. Subsequently, the State of Missouri decided to use the building to consolidate administrative offices and services.

A design competition was held to choose a plan for the restoration of the building. The program for the competition called for restoration of the exterior of the building, remodeling the interior, and construction of an annex. The annex covers three-quarters of the city block on which the Wainwright Building is located. Three stories high with a brick facade, the annex clearly matches the facade materials of the original.

Other work included the construction of a new elevator tower and the conversion of the interior light well of the U-shaped Wainwright Building into an atrium. A large public plaza is part of the annex. This combination of a new building with an old and historic building has created a handsome and vital new complex that consolidates many previous scattered state agencies.

Nineteenth-Century Cotton Export Building to Foundation Offices

The Hendley Building, built in 1859 as cotton export offices, is the last and oldest commercial structure on the row in the east end of Galveston's historic Strand area. In 1968, the building was threatened with demolition and was purchased by the local preservation organization, the Galveston Historical Foundation. More than a decade later, the Foundation decided to move their offices to the building.

A report on the structural condition of the building indicated severe problems including a wall badly bowing out 10 inches. Options for stabilizing the wall included rebuilding the wall or buttressing it. Both options would cost about the same. The architects for the project developed a system to buttress the wall that solved more than the structural problem. A steel framework was erected and tensioned against the bowing wall to stabilize it. This gridwork ran the entire length of the building creating a 100-foot-long buttress system approximately 5 feet deep. New building services, including HVAC and electrical, were placed in this new space, saving the original space for a historic renovation, including the retention of all original interior walls.

The Hendley Building in Galveston, Texas was built in 1859 as cotton export offices. It is the last building on the row in the east end of the city's historic Strand area. A buttress system was devised to stabilize a badly deteriorated exposed party wall. Photographic credit: Taft Architects.

CREDITS
NAME & LOCATION: Hendley Building, Galveston, Texas
ARCHITECT: Taft Architects, Houston, Texas
DEVELOPER: Galveston Historical Foundation, Galveston, Texas

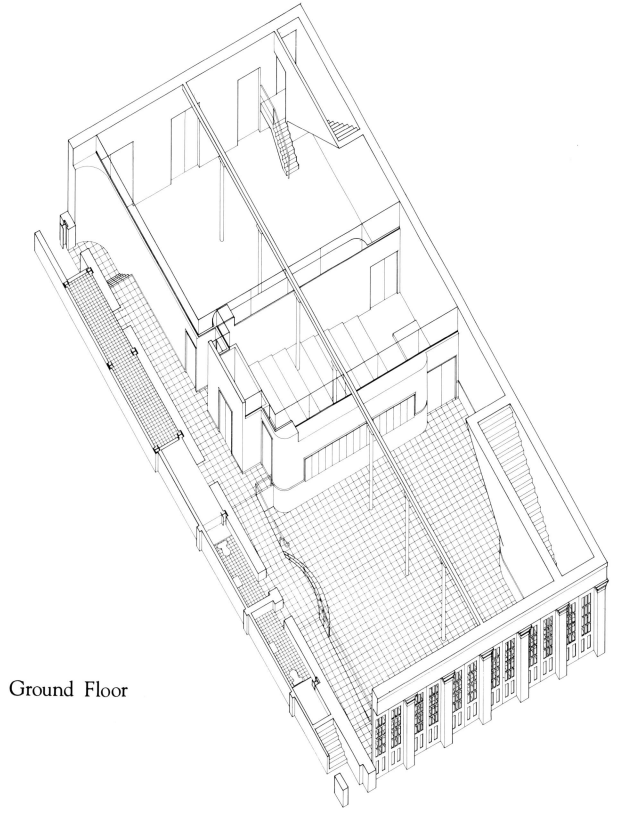

Ground Floor

The buttress system runs the length of the building, approximately 100 feet and is 5 feet deep. New building services, including HVAC and electrical, were placed in the new space created by the buttress system. Drawing credit: Taft Architects.

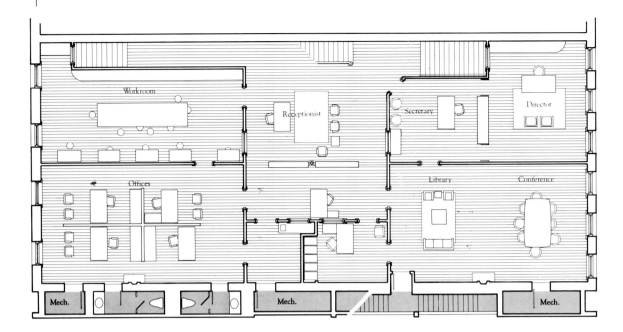

Second Floor Plan

The buttress system allows the original features of the historic building, including the walls, to be retained in their original configuration. Drawing credit: Taft Architects.

The new addition to the Hendley Building makes careful use of color to blend with the existing historic setting. The offices of the Galveston Historical Foundation are thus in a historic setting with all the conveniences of modern office space.

Upgrading a 1970s Office Tower in the 1980s

Age is not necessarily a determining factor in all office building rehabilitations. The InterFirst II building, built in Dallas, Texas in the mid-1970s, was a 56-story curtain wall building of approximately 1.7 million square feet of space. By the mid-1980s the building had developed two major problems. First, a seal failure on the glazed exterior caused oxidation of the coating. The second was a perceptual problem. David Dillon, architecture critic for the *Dallas Morning News*, labeled the InterFirst II building, "one of Dallas' bench-mark bad buildings" that was "quintessentially dumb."[1]

To solve these problems, the new owners of the building turned to the architectural firm of Skidmore, Owings and Merrill who completely revamped the curtain wall facade of the building. A new granite base was added to the building to give it a more human scale and to provide an illusion of support

[1] David Dillon, "Clunky InterFirst II Becomes Fashionable Renaissance Tower," *The Dallas Morning News*, November 1, 1987, p. 1C.

The InterFirst II building was a 56-story curtain wall building built in Dallas, Texas in the mid-1970s. By the mid-1980s the building had developed a number of problems, not the least of which was a bad image.

CREDITS
NAME & LOCATION: Renaissance Tower, Dallas, Texas
ARCHITECT: Skidmore, Owings & Merrill, Chicago, Illinois
DEVELOPER: The Prudential Insurance Company of America

for a new glass curtain wall. Visual variety was added to the curtain wall by using colored panels of green, blue, and silver glass that highlighted the original "X" bracing of the tower's structural system. A new roof structure consisting of five pyramidal towers was added to provide definition. The lobby was extensively remodeled, and the exterior courtyard was given new life by adding an 81-foot-high glass pyramid structure enclosing a food court and patio. The makeover of the structure also includes an underground retail development component. The rejuvenation has resulted in a building that is much more competitive in the Dallas real estate market.

A new granite base adds further definition to the curtain wall. An exterior courtyard, including a glass pyramid housing a food court and a patio, encourages pedestrian traffic around the building.

84

In its renovation, the curtain wall was revamped, different colored glass panels were used to highlight the structural bracing system of the building, and a new roof structure was added to provide definition.

Medical Office in Mansion

In Bristol, Connecticut part of a former mansion has been converted into medical offices. The mansion, called Beleden, was the home of William E. Sessions of the Sessions Company, a nationally prominent watch and clock manufacturer in the nineteenth century. The medical office is located in "found" space in the basement of the structure that had originally served as furnace, coal storage, and laundry rooms. To create a modern medical office in this space, all of the existing partitions were removed, modern mechanical systems were installed, and new windows and an entryway were created. The entryway, located at the rear of the structure to preserve the character of the

Underused space in the basement of the historic Sessions Mansion in Bristol, Connecticut has been refurbished as a modern medical office. The entrance to the new suite of offices uses materials that match those of the historic structure. All of the improvements are hidden from view from the street, preserving the architectural integrity of the mansion. Photographic credit: Gilley-Hickel Architects.

CREDITS
NAME & LOCATION: Sessions Mansion, Bristol, Connecticut
ARCHITECT: Gilley-Hinkel Architects, Bristol, Connecticut
OWNER: Dr. Steven Wernick, Bristol, Connecticut

property, is almost completely below grade. The wall along the entryway is made of brick to match the original materials of the house. From the street, all of the improvements to accommodate a modern medical office are hidden from view.

Historic Office Building More Than Doubles Its Size

The 16-story Mid-Continent Building in downtown Tulsa, Oklahoma was built in 1918 and is listed on the National Register of Historic Places. The building, designed in a Tudor Gothic style, has an ornate terra cotta facade. In the early 1980s, the building underwent a major renovation that included an addition that more than doubled the size of the original historic structure. The addition, designed to match the original, was built on an adjacent parking lot and rises a total of 36 stories. At the sixteenth story, it cantilevers out 40 feet over the original building, then continues upward for an additional 20 floors. The new building uses prefabricated terra cotta panels to replicate the historic facade. Although the original building and the new addition are two

CREDITS
NAME & LOCATION: Mid-Continent Tower, Tulsa, Oklahoma
ARCHITECT/ENGINEER: HTB, Inc., Oklahoma City, Oklahoma
OWNER: Reading and Bates

A major addition more than doubled the size of the historic Mid-Continent Building in downtown Tulsa, Oklahoma. The new addition was built on land adjacent to the historic building and cantilevers out above the original structure. Photographic credit: Jon B. Petersen Photography, Inc.

The exterior material of the new addition copies the ornate Tudor Gothic terra cotta facade of the historic structure. Photographic credit: Jon B. Petersen Photography, Inc.

separate structures, they appear, because of the unifying facade element, as a single building. The entire 320,000-square foot project was rechristened the Mid-Continent Tower.

College Campus Becomes Office Campus

In Baltimore, Maryland a nineteenth-century college campus has been transformed into the offices of a major finance and insurance company. McAuley Hall, built in the 1920s, was the major focal point of the campus; today, it remains the centerpiece of the office complex and serves as an education and computer center. A major addition to the building houses the company's data processing center. An octagonal structure built in 1885 serves as the hospitality and reception center for the complex. The former college athletic facilities were refurbished and are now used by employees of the company. The college campus provides sufficient space for automobile parking, which is located adjacent to the data processing center.

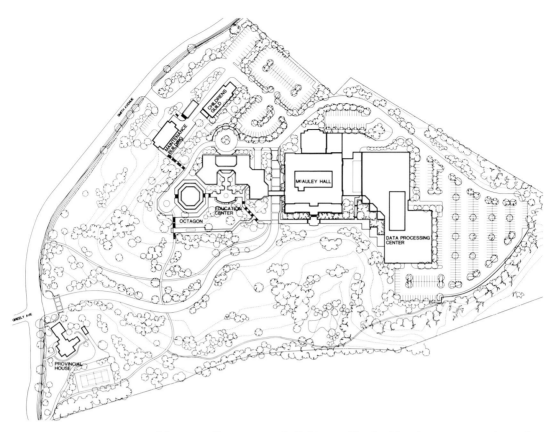

A former college campus in Baltimore, Maryland has been converted into offices for USF&G, a major insurance company. A new addition houses the data processing operations of the company, and a new parking area was built. Drawing credit: RTKL Associates, Inc.

CREDITS
NAME & LOCATION: USF&G Mount Washington Center, Baltimore, Maryland
ARCHITECT: RTKL Associates, Inc., Bernard J. Wulff, AIA, Principal in Charge, Baltimore, Maryland
DEVELOPER: United States Fidelity and Guaranty Company, Baltimore, Maryland

McAuley Hall, a 1920s college building, and an 1885 octagonal structure have been retained as part of the transformation of the campus. Photographic credit: RTKL Associates Inc. and Hedrick-Blessing.

School to Offices

The George W. Guthrie School in Wilkes-Barre, Pennsylvania was built in 1915 as a school for "backward" children. It was closed as a school in the early 1970s and was used as a storage facility for 10 years, after which it was declared surplus property and sold at auction. The building was acquired by InterMetro Industries Corporation and was rehabilitated to serve as their corporate headquarters.

The exterior was repaired and restored using in-kind materials including replacement of the roof with new slate and duplication of the window sashes. Modern double-glazed windows were substituted for the deteriorated original windows. On the interior many of the partitions that had defined the original classrooms were removed to create large open spaces that could be configured to suit a particular corporate department. The original double-loaded corridor system was retained, as was the service space parallel to each classroom that had originally served to house cloakrooms and mechanical functions. These

The former Guthrie School in Wilkes-Barre, Pennsylvania, is now the corporate headquarters of InterMetro Industries. A three-story stone and steel trellis marks the entrance to the new offices. Photographic credit: Christopher H. Barone.

CREDITS
NAME & LOCATION: InterMetro Industries Corporation Headquarters, Wilkes-Barre, Pennsylvania
ARCHITECT: Bohlin Powell Larkin Cywinski, Peter Q. Bohlin, FAIA, Principal in Charge, Wilkes-Barre, Pennsylvania
MECHANICAL/ELECTRICAL/STRUCTURAL CONSULTANTS: Utility Engineers
DEVELOPER: InterMetro Industries Corporation, Wilkes-Barre, Pennsylvania

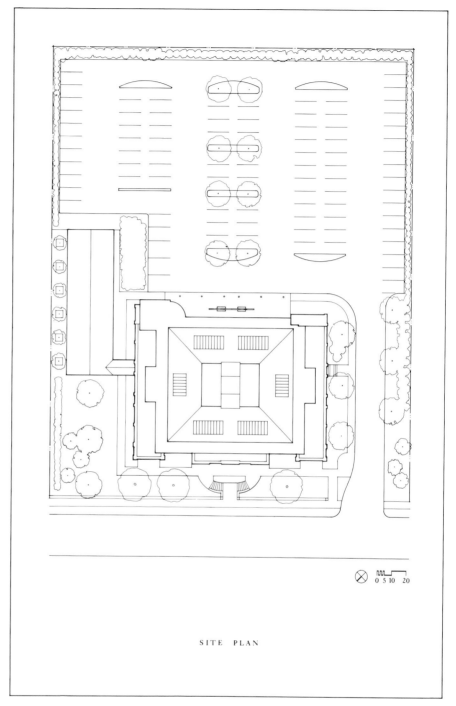

SITE PLAN

A parking area has been created from former playgrounds behind the original building resulting in a change of the building's primary entrance facing the parking area. Drawing credit: Bohlin Powell Larkin Cywinski.

service areas now support office functions including photocopy equipment, files, and supplies. Additionally, the elevator, bathrooms, and janitorial facilities were also housed in the original service area. The stairways were sheathed with glass partitions for fire safety, thus preserving the original character of the school corridors.

Parking considerations played an important role in the overall plan. A new parking area was located on the former school playground at the rear of the building necessitating a new rear entrance. This new entrance, which forms the central element in the building's reorientation, is marked by a three-story stone and steel trellis.

The first three floors of the building serve as general office areas for the corporation; the interior finishes and molding were restored. The large windows of the school building were retained and provide an important source of light for office workers. The fourth floor, which had originally served as the attic space in the school, was refurbished as the executive offices for the firm. These offices make use of existing skylights located on the hipped roof.

6

Conversion to Institutional Use

Institutions come in all shapes and sizes—as do their buildings and their building requirements. (Institution is used here to mean nonprofit organizations that, for purposes of this chapter, own or maintain their own building or facility, for example, museums, universities, and churches.) This chapter describes how many different building types have been reused to meet the needs of various institutions.

The useful conversion of an existing building by an institution often directly benefits the public through new public uses of derelict or underused buildings. Institutional use of existing buildings almost invariably attracts people, and this activity is an important product of this type of conversion. For example, the San Antonio Museum of Art is housed in a former brewery. The conversion of this building not only preserved an architecturally distinctive building, but brought new life to a section of the city that formerly did not have a great deal of street activity.

In a number of cities throughout the country, small and medium-sized nonprofit organizations have banded together to buy or lease space as a group. Such an approach can generate an economy of scale that allows a nonprofit organization to occupy space that it otherwise would not be able to afford. For example, a nineteenth-century multistory stable building that somehow miraculously survived in the midst of Washington, D.C.'s booming downtown real estate market was recently converted into the Stable Arts Center and is now the home to a number of arts administration and performing arts organizations.

The public use of institutional conversions demands careful attention to accessibility requirements. To some degree, modifications of an existing building to achieve accessibility should be the starting point in the design and engineering phase of the conversion. Extensive structural modifications such as stairways, elevators, new entrances, fire routing, and delivery bays may be necessary to achieve accessibility.

Conversion of an existing building by an institution for its own use can achieve a number of different objectives. Rehabilitation is normally more

A number of arts administration and performing arts organizations in Washington, D.C. are now housed in a former stable building, appropriately called the Stables Art Center. Photographic credit: Peter H. Smith.

economical than building anew, and it generally takes less time to bring the building on line. This is an important consideration that often makes old buildings attractive, especially for nonprofit organizations. Older buildings that have large expanses of open space readily lend themselves to a variety of uses such as office space, exhibit space, workshop, and meeting areas. Older buildings help define a sense of place and are often valuable visual resources of a community. In this sense, the buildings can help provide an identity for an organization. Reuse of an old building can help a nonprofit organization achieve goodwill within a community.

Brewery to Art Museum

The Lone Star Brewery in San Antonio, Texas was built in 1904 and closed in 1925. Today, the building has been imaginatively adapted as the new home of the San Antonio Museum of Art. By the time the museum acquired the building in 1970, the brewery had been subdivided into individual industrial enterprises such as auto repair shops and was in an advanced state of deterioration.

The brewery building is primarily Romanesque Revival in style, but an early Gothic parapet makes the building resemble a medieval walled town. The brewery consists of two towers connected by a two-story building. The two towers were connected on the upper levels by a pedestrian bridge. The original construction of the brewery included cast iron columns and steel beams that supported a vaulted floor system of brick and concrete. The exterior walls are of heavy load-bearing masonry construction.

The San Antonio Museum of Art in San Antonio, Texas is housed in the former Lone Star Brewery built in 1904. The unusual architecture and shape of the former brewery were the major design forces in adapting the building to a museum.
Photographic credit: Nick Wheeler/Wheeler Photographics.

CREDITS
NAME & LOCATION: San Antonio Museum of Art, San Antonio, Texas
ARCHITECT: Cambridge Seven Associates, Inc., Cambridge, Massachusetts in association
    with Chumney, Jones & Kell, Inc., San Antonio, Texas

The project architects used the unusual shape and layout of the building as the major force for their design. Since there was no basement, the new mechanical equipment was located on the top of each of the flanking towers. This allowed each tower to provide services within its framework and, at the same time, to remain separate from the museum functions of the building.

Slow-moving, glass-enclosed elevators in each tower provide full accessibility to all floors of the museum and give passengers a glimpse of the installation in each of the galleries as the elevators rise and descend. A new glass-enclosed walkway was constructed between the two towers to provide complete circulation throughout the museum. Gallery space is located in the towers, and the connecting building houses the lobby, gift shop, and auditorium.

A major change in the exterior appearance of the building occurred when the original wood window sashes were replaced with anodized aluminum frames. The wood sashes had substantially deteriorated, and energy requirements and the program needs of the museum dictated the use of the new frames.

The main brewery building provides approximately 50,000 square feet of museum space. The brewery property consists of eight buildings, all of which have been acquired by the museum and are used for a variety of purposes.

Slow moving glass-enclosed elevators are located in each of the towers of the building. They give riders a glimpse of the installations on each floor. Photographic credit: Nick Wheeler/Wheeler Photographics.

The project, which is located along the San Antonio River, is connected to the city's famous Riverwalk and has proved to be an important catalyst for other revitalization projects in the general vicinity.

Historic College Building Given New Life on Campus

At DePauw University in Greencastle, Indiana, the East College building stands as the centerpiece of the campus. It was completed in 1882 after 13 years of construction, and is said to have an architectural design that provides something for everyone. The building employs Gothic arches, Tudor gables, a French mansard roof, and Italianate columns.

By the mid-1970s, because of extensive deterioration, the building faced an uncertain future. A restoration feasibility study was undertaken that indicated that the building could be successfully restored and again serve as a vital and integral part of campus life. The work on the building included the

The historically significant East College Building at DePauw University in Greencastle, Indiana, completed in 1882, has been restored as the eclectic architectural centerpiece of the campus.

CREDITS
NAME & LOCATION: East College, DePauw University, Greencastle, Indiana
ARCHITECT: James Architects and Engineers, Inc., H. Roll McLaughlin, FAIA, Principal Architect, Indianapolis, Indiana

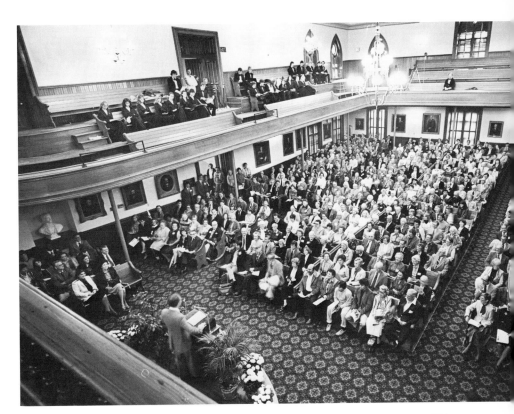

The auditorium in East College was restored using historical photographic evidence. Photographic credit: Dave Repp.

installation of entirely new mechanical and electrical systems as well as some structural stabilization work on badly deteriorated sections of the building. The exterior of the building was fully restored as was the original auditorium space using historical photographic evidence.

The original interior walls were retained and movable partitions were added in some areas to accommodate new space needs. A sprinkler system permitted the retention of the original open wood stairways. Handicapped access is provided by a lift to the basement level of the building, and an elevator provides transportation to all levels of the building. Today, the building is once again the eclectic architectural centerpiece of the campus.

Private School Expansion

A shingle-style residential building has served a pivotal role in the life of the Dublin School in Dublin, New Hampshire. Called the Main House, the building first served as the home of the school's founder and then as the main dormitory and dining hall of the school. In the mid-1980s, the school needed more room, and this centerpiece of the campus was expanded. The size of the building was doubled to approximately 10,000 square feet to include a student lounge, snack bar, locker rooms, and athletic store by expanding the building down the steeply sloped site. Today, the Main House continues to serve the students and faculty of the Dublin School and has been awarded an Honor Award by the New Hampshire Chapter of the American Institute of Architects.

The shingle-style Main House at the Dublin School in Dublin, New Hampshire had originally been built as the home of the school's founder. A recent expansion program nearly doubled the size of the house to include new facilities for students. Photographic credit: Richard M. Monahon, Jr., AIA.

CREDITS
NAME & LOCATION: *Main House, Dublin School, Dublin, New Hampshire*
ARCHITECT: *Richard M. Monahon, Jr., AIA Peterborough, New Hampshire*

The new library and learning center at Colby-Sawyer College in New London, New Hampshire is located in two former nineteenth-century dairy barns. The rehabilitation work included the construction of new basements beneath the barns.
Drawing credit: The Burley Partnership.

CREDITS
NAME & LOCATION: Susan-Colgate Cleveland Library, Colby-Sawyer College, New London, New Hampshire
ARCHITECT: The Burley Partnership, Waitsfield, Vermont
STRUCTURAL ENGINEER: Spiegel and Zamecnik, Washington, D.C.

The interior of the new library makes effective use of the structural wood framing system that was part of the original barns.

Barn into College Library

Conversion of older buildings to new uses sometimes results in strange bedfellows. Such is the case at an innovative conversion at Colby-Sawyer College in New London, New Hampshire. The college had the opportunity to acquire a farm adjacent to its main campus. A feasibility study indicated that two mid-nineteenth-century dairy barns on the farm could be adapted for use as the college's library. To carry out the plan, the barns were moved so that basements could be constructed. The main entryway into the library is through the silo, and reading spaces were constructed in lofts supported by timber framing on the upper levels of the barn. New sheds were constructed on the side to provide additional reading and study areas.

The former post office and federal office building in downtown Buffalo, New York has become the new campus of Erie Community College. The building, completed in 1900, was designed in a Gothic style and includes a 250-foot-high tower and a large interior atrium. Photographic credit: Patricia Layman Bazelon.

CREDITS
NAME & LOCATION: Erie Community
  College: City Campus, Buffalo,
  New York
ARCHITECT: Cannon, Inc., Buffalo,
  New York

City Post Office to Community College Facility

In Buffalo, New York the former post office and federal office building has been imaginatively converted to the downtown campus of Erie Community College. The post office, completed in 1900, was designed in a Gothic style with a 250-foot tower and a large interior atrium space used to sort mail. The 100-foot-high and 12,000-square foot atrium serves as the major organizational element in the reuse of the building. It now includes an auditorium, library, and cafeteria for the college. The skylight was replaced to increase energy efficiency. Fire regulations required the use of sprinklers in the open atrium. College classrooms are located on the upper floors of the building, which formerly housed federal offices, including justice facilities. The ornate paneling in the courtrooms has been retained in the new use of the building. The building contains 225,000 gross square feet of space, enough to accommodate all of the needs of the college's 2,000 students.

Some of the classrooms in the building retain the ornate paneling of the former federal courtrooms. Photographic credit: Patricia Layman Bazelon.

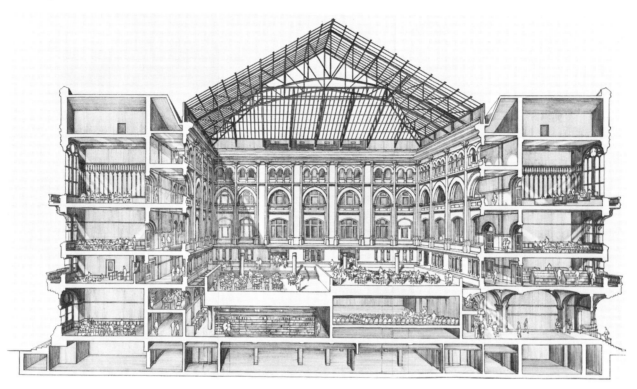

The large interior atrium of the old post office contains an auditorium, cafeteria, and library. The former mail sorting floor is the major organizing element of the building interior. Drawing credit: Cannon, Inc.

Three Landmarks on the University of Chicago Campus: 1890 University Anthropology Museum to Business School

At the University of Chicago, a building designed in 1890 by Henry Ives Cobb as an anthropological history museum has been transformed into the Graduate School of Business. Although designed as a museum facility, the building was never totally devoted to this use, having housed a lecture hall and office spaces for more than 75 years. The conversion to the business school demanded significant changes to accommodate the school's specialized needs.

The building had to accommodate additional office space for both faculty and administrative personnel, student space requirements, and computer facilities. At the same time, the University resolved to preserve the important historic character of the building. Facilities for the school's mainframe computer and distribution system throughout the building required fully separate environmental controls. Major structural changes were made to accommodate additional office space. The high ceiling of the museum between the first and second floors allowed the installation of a mezzanine level with a cutout at the central lobby preserving the original character of the space. The third floor was removed and replaced with two new floors that were designed to the original scale of the building.

Decorative elements throughout the building were restored wherever possible. The public areas of the building were retained at their original scale. An open stairwell that extends the full height of the building is the principal source of circulation within the building.

A former anthropological museum, built in 1890, at the University of Chicago has become the home of the Graduate School of Business. Photographic credit: Harr, Hedrich-Blessing.

CREDITS
NAME & LOCATION: Walker Museum/Graduate School of Business, University of Chicago, Chicago, Illinois
ARCHITECT: Nagle, Hartray & Associates, Architects/Planners, Chicago, Illinois
ASSOCIATE ARCHITECT: Harold H. Hellman, FAIA, Chicago, Illinois

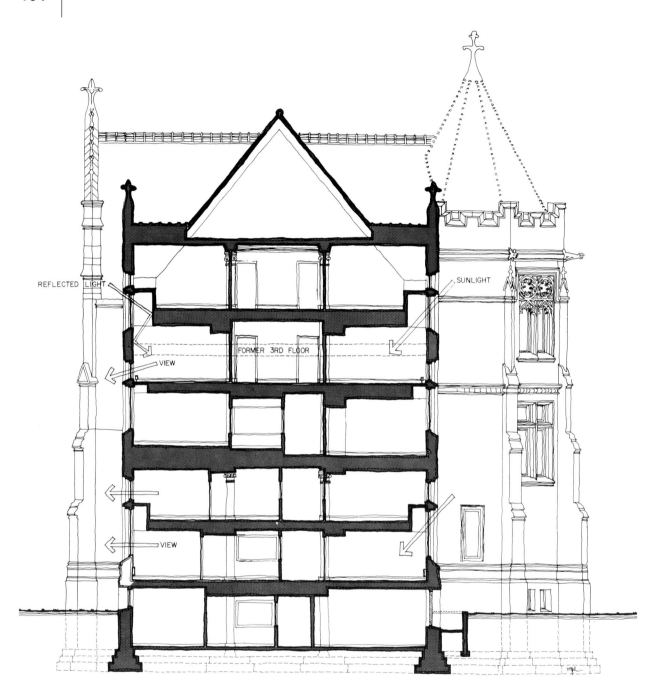

REFLECTED LIGHT

SUNLIGHT

FORMER 3RD FLOOR

VIEW

VIEW

TRANSVERSE SECTION

Floor levels in the building were altered to accommodate the specialized needs of the business school including new environmental controls for increased computer use.

Upgrading a Victorian Era University Concert Hall

The Leon Mandel Assembly Hall, a 1,000-seat auditorium on the University of Chicago campus, has faithfully served the university community as a performance space since it was completed in 1903. Mandel Hall is one of a group of surrounding buildings on the campus, called the Tower Group of Buildings, that was designed by the architectural firm of Shepley, Rutan and Coolidge.

CREDITS
NAME & LOCATION: Leon Mandel Assembly Hall, University of Chicago, Chicago, Illinois
ARCHITECT: Skidmore, Owings & Merrill, Architects, Chicago, Illinois
ASSOCIATE ARCHITECT: Harold H. Hellman, FAIA, Chicago, Illinois

---

Leon Mandel Assembly Hall at the University of Chicago was built in 1903. A major upgrading of the building has been carried out to incorporate contemporary technology for theatre and musical performances. Photographic credit: Howard N. Kaplan, Architectural Photography.

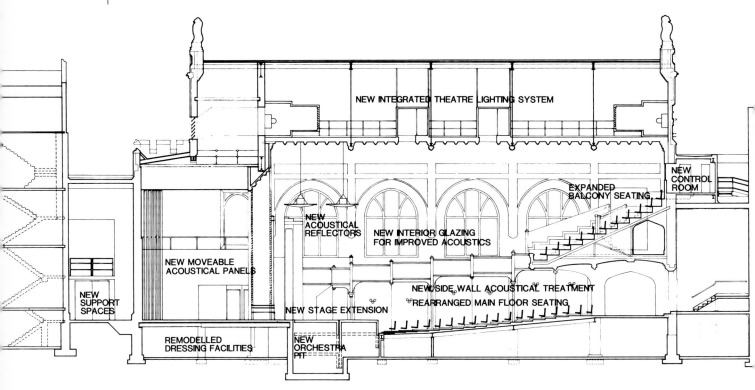

Major work was undertaken in the stage area: a new and enlarged music platform was installed, hydraulic lifts allow reconfiguration of the stage, and acoustical properties of the hall were upgraded. Drawing credit: Skidmore, Owings & Merrill.

In the late 1970s, the University began a program to upgrade Mandel Hall and to incorporate contemporary technology for theatre and musical performance capabilities.

Mandel Hall had few physical alterations in its first 75 years. Major attention was paid to the stage area; a new and enlarged music platform was installed in front of the proscenium arch. Hydraulic lifts can change the height of the platform, which can be completely lowered to floor level to create additional seating. Dressing rooms were relocated to a level below the stage. A small addition was constructed directly behind the stage to accommodate a new loading dock, work area, and storage space. The projection, sound, and light equipment, which had been located amid balcony seats, were moved behind the balcony wall.

Careful attention was paid to upgrading the acoustical properties of the hall to substantially reduce exterior noise, to aid performers in hearing one another, and to improve the acoustical properties of the hall for large instrumental and choral groups. As part of the overall program, audience seating and sightlines were improved. The interior decoration of the hall was largely restored using original colors.

Reworking a Reworked University Building

The University of Chicago's Goodspeed Hall, designed by Henry Ives Cobb in 1892, was originally built as a residence for divinity students. In 1920 the building was completely gutted for use as a library. The remodeling work was

At the University of Chicago, Goodspeed Hall was originally built in 1892 as a dormitory for divinity students. In 1920 the building was remodeled and became a library. In 1980, the building underwent another remodeling and became home to the University's Music Department. Photographic credit: Skidmore, Owings & Merrill.

CREDITS
NAME & LOCATION: Goodspeed Hall, University of Chicago, Chicago, Illinois
ARCHITECT: Skidmore, Owings & Merrill, Architects, Chicago, Illinois
ASSOCIATE ARCHITECT: Harold H. Hellman, FAIA, Chicago, Illinois

extensive and involved removal of the original floors and the installation of a new steel structure within the walls of the building to support the library's high loads. In the late 1970s, as part of a major university program, Goodspeed Hall, along with Mandel Hall, was extensively remodeled for use by the university's Music Department.

The 1920s structural system was reused in this reincarnation of the building. The music department required the design of acoustically isolated rooms—shielded from other areas on the same floor and from rooms above and below—that could be used for teaching and for practice by the music faculty and students. Acoustical isolation was achieved by isolating the mechanical duct runs, and by using special floors and doors. The walls between rooms are constructed of concrete block with furred-out dry wall on both sides. Insulation between the studs increases acoustical isolation. Additionally, double-glazed windows and drapes help baffle exterior noise infiltration. A recital space was constructed in an abutting building and is connected to the main music department by a stair and ramp.

Although it was difficult initially for the music faculty to envision how a dormitory became a library and was about to become the new home of the music department, the building has won considerable praise following its completion in 1980.

The needs of the Music Department required acoustically isolated rooms for teaching and practice. This was achieved by isolating the mechanical ducts, and using special floors and doors, double-glazed windows, and concrete block walls furred out and filled with insulation. Photographic credit: Howard N. Kaplan, Architectural Photography.

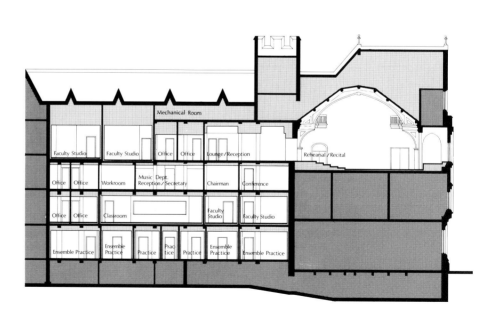

Rehearsal and recital space for the music department is located in an abutting building that was joined to Goodspeed Hall to create the needed space.

Goodspeed Hall

Section

Classics Building

VA Hospital Gets New Entrance

The Veterans' Administration Hospital in Sioux Falls, South Dakota was originally designed in a collegiate gothic architectural vocabulary. A recent expansion added 79,000 square feet to the original hospital. The new addition is built into the sloping site of the hospital facility and preserves the integrity of the facade of the main building.

The addition includes a new main entrance that provides full handicapped accessibility. Stairs were also built around the new entrance to provide access to an additional entrance as well as a pedestrian plaza. New parking facilities were included adjacent to the main entrance. The materials of the new addition, brick and limestone, echo the materials of the original structure. The new addition, which carefully makes use of the topography of the site, includes extensive landscaping around the entrance.

An expansion and new entrance to the Veterans' Administration Hospital in Sioux Falls, South Dakota uses the sloping topography of the site. The new parking area is screened from the main hospital facility. Photographic credit: Architectural Images.

CREDITS
NAME & LOCATION: Veterans' Administration Hospital Addition and Renovation,
   Sioux Falls, South Dakota
ARCHITECT: Spitznagel, Architects, Engineers, Planners, Sioux Falls, South Dakota

The Radcliffe Quadrangle in Cambridge, Massachusetts has been redefined to become part of the Harvard University North and Cabot Houses. New entrances were developed to preserve the open space of the quadrangle; a new dining hall uses a curved glass wall providing views of quadrangle activities. Photographic credit: Steve Rosenthal.

CREDITS
NAME & LOCATION: North and Cabot Houses, Radcliffe Quadrangle, Harvard University, Cambridge, Massachusetts
ARCHITECT: Notter Finegold + Alexander, Inc., Boston, Massachusetts
LANDSCAPE ARCHITECT: Carol R. Johnson & Associates, Cambridge, Massachusetts
STRUCTURAL ENGINEERS: Souza, True & Partners, Boston, Massachusetts
INTERIOR DESIGN: JGL Interiors, Boston, Massachusetts
MECHANICAL ENGINEERS: Thompson Consultants, Inc., Marion, Massachusetts
ELECTRICAL ENGINEERS: Thompson Engineering Co., Inc., Boston, Massachusetts

College Quadrangle Preserved and Enhanced

Following the merger of Radcliffe and Harvard in Cambridge, Massachusetts, 10 dormitories surrounding a Radcliffe quadrangle were redefined as two "Houses" to become part of the Harvard House system. The dormitories were renovated to create more efficient use of space. Underused attic space was converted into new dormitory space including some two-level suites. At one end of the quadrangle, a new dining hall was created on the lower level of one of the buildings, featuring a curved glass wall that opens up a vista to the entire quadrangle area. Throughout the area, new entrances to the buildings were developed to preserve the open space of the quadrangle and offer full views of activity in the enclosed space. Infill construction was used to unify two of the older buildings on the site and create a new main entryway from the quadrangle into one of the new houses.

7

Interior
Spaces

Although the exterior of a building—its architectural style, form, and materials—receives the most critical attention, the building's interior—the rooms, corridors, classrooms, and assembly areas—ultimately determines its success or failure. The interior dictates how and how well the occupants—workers, students, residents, and so on—respond to the building. Living and working take place on the inside of a building and, therefore, it is within the building that people find a satisfactory or unsatisfactory environment. In this sense, the interior environment is the most important part of any building. The interior can be private, such as a home or corporate office, or public, such as a museum or office building lobby.

Whereas the building exterior is relatively fixed—it is a major undertaking to "rearrange" the location of windows on the facade—interiors are the most changeable part of the architecture of a building. Structural considerations of the exterior demand primary attention, whereas interior partitions and walls, if they are not load bearing, can be rearranged with relative impunity.

Interior spaces frequently change to reflect new uses, new ownership, fads, custom, technological advances, and personal preference. Technological changes that have occurred in heating and air conditioning over the last few decades have had a great effect on the flexibility of interior spaces in new and existing buildings.

Interiors often can be as important a visual resource as the building exterior. For example, the picture palaces of the early twentieth century were consciously designed to provide a fantasy environment for the movie goer. Indeed, in some instances, important interior spaces, such as in movie palaces, have been designated as landmarks.

When adapting a building to a new use, prominent interior features and spatial arrangements should be assessed for significance and retention. Different building types have distinctive interior features that contribute to their significance. For example, the structural system of a mill building is an important consideration for creating expansive space.

Guernsey Hall, a 40-room mansion in Princeton, New Jersey, was converted into five condominium units. The original sequence of rooms as well as the original detailing were retained in the conversion. Photographic credit: Otto Baitz.

CREDITS
NAME & LOCATION: Guernsey Hall, Princeton, New Jersey
ARCHITECTS: Short and Ford, Architects, Princeton, New Jersey
DEVELOPER: Guernsey Hall, Inc., Princeton, New Jersey

In residential structures, the spatial or room arrangements are an important interior element that defines the sense of use of the building. For example, Guernsey Hall in Princeton, New Jersey, a landmark project of the late 1970s, was converted from a 40-room mansion to five condominium apartments. The interior of the building was redesigned so that the original sequence of rooms was retained along with original detailing. The exterior of the building was restored as was the central stairway, which featured trompe l'oeil walls and ceiling.

Finishes and detailing are also significant interior features of a building. Typically, late nineteenth- and early twentieth-century office buildings had ornate and elaborate lobbies and entrances. When possible, such detailing should be retained because it provides visual richness as well as evidence of the past life of a building.

Interior arrangements can be relatively easy to change. A room can be completely transformed simply by rearranging its furniture. The addition of partitions can alter the spatial perception of an interior environment. The elimination of partitions and walls can create a completely different effect.

Local zoning regulations have a considerable impact on the conversion of an existing building from one type of use to another. In large measure, zoning codes are aimed at separating incompatible uses so that, for example, an iron foundry is not located next to a hospital. To the extent that zoning codes control the use of a building, they determine what takes place on the interior.

Unused or underused space on the inside of a building can often be converted to productive space, without physically enlarging a building. For example, a homeowner can convert the attic or basement to productive living space. New space can also be created. For example, in a building with very tall ceilings it is often possible to create a new floor level. Similarly, large expanses of open space can be subdivided to make a new spatial arrangement. Cutting through a floor can create dramatic interior space.

When mixing the interiors of old and new buildings, circulation and accessibility are important considerations that are covered by codes for fire, safety, and accessibility for the handicapped. As the following examples demonstrate, it is often a considerable design challenge to maintain an interior's significant features, and still meet code requirements.

Nineteenth-Century Mill Becomes Professional Offices

In northern New Jersey, a stone grist mill, built in 1842 (following the Oliver Evans principles for an automated milling system), has been converted into the offices of a 20-person architectural firm. The mill is a designated historic landmark and contains 5,300 square feet. The original milling equipment was preserved *in situ* and provides both visual diversity for the office environment as well as a museum of milling technology.

The mill race has been preserved and functions as a heat exchanger for the heat pump for climate control of the building. A central feature of the reuse scheme is an open stairwell from the basement to the third and top floor of the mill, which permits visual contact throughout the building and contributes to the open office layout of the firm. Drafting studios are located on the third floor, with conference rooms located on the mezzanine level and administrative offices located on the second floor. The first floor, which houses most of the mill equipment, functions as a museum.

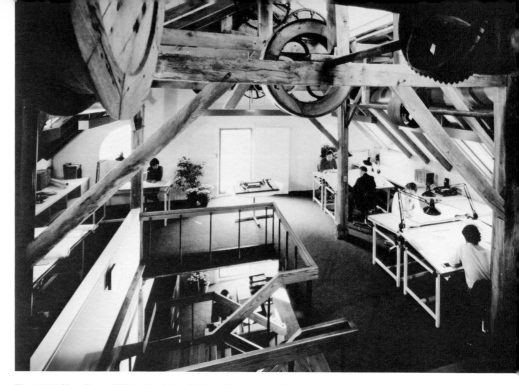

The 1842 Van Dorn Mill in Basking Ridge, New Jersey has been remodeled as architectural offices. The original mill equipment has been preserved in situ. The open stairwell provides circulation and communication throughout the building. Photographic credit: Ashod Kassabian.

CREDITS
NAME & LOCATION: *Van Dorn Mill, Offices of Haines Lundberg Waehler, Basking Ridge, New Jersey*
ARCHITECT: *Haines Lundberg Waehler, New York, New York*

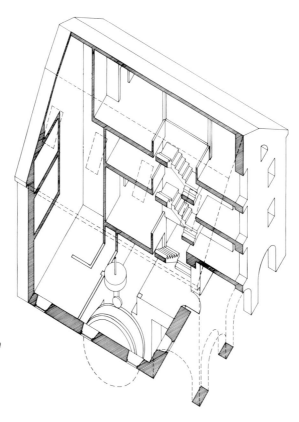

Axonometric view of the Van Dorn Mill. The first floor is devoted to an exhibition of milling; the other floors contain architectural offices. Photographic credit: Haines Lundberg Waehler.

Warehouse Complex Converted to Specialty Shopping and Residences

The Toronto Terminal warehouse in Toronto, Ontario, built in 1926, has been transformed into a specialty shopping facility with offices, condominiums, and rental residential apartments. The reuse scheme was the result of a competition sponsored by the city's harborfront authority in 1980. The site includes 12.5 acres and well over a million square feet of space. As part of the project, four floors of condominium apartments were added to the top of the warehouse building to provide space for 72 units.

On the inside of the structure, two large atria were created by removing the floors, while retaining the structural columns of the original building. The atria not only create comprehensible circulation patterns throughout the huge building, but provide views and light for the offices on the interiors of the upper floors. Circulation can be segregated on the upper floors of the building between shoppers, office workers, and residents by different banks of elevators. Retail spaces on the ground floor not only open onto the interior of the atria, but can also be opened to the outdoors during good weather.

The Toronto Terminal warehouse in Toronto, Ontario, originally built in 1926, has been transformed into the Queen's Quay Terminal and includes over a million square feet of office, retail, and residential space. Four floors of apartments were added to the top of the terminal to create additional residential space. Photographic credit: Peter H. Smeallie.

CREDITS
NAME & LOCATION: Queen's Quay Terminal, Toronto, Ontario, Canada
ARCHITECT: Zeidler Roberts Partnership, Toronto, Ontario, Canada
DEVELOPER: Olympia & York Development Ltd., Toronto, Ontario, Canada

Two large atria were created on the interior by removing the flooring while retaining the structural system of columns in the original building. Photographic credit: Peter H. Smeallie.

Wholesale Gift Showroom from Concrete Warehouse

The historic Blake, Moffitt, and Towne Building, a four-story concrete warehouse built in the 1920s, has been remodeled as the San Francisco Gift Center. The large building contains 300,000 square feet of wholesale showroom space and a five-story central atrium. The atrium space was formerly the loading dock area for the warehouse and is used as a restaurant during the day and a special events space in the evening. Balconies overlook the atrium space and the skylights on the atrium are retractable.

A former horse barn has been converted into a weekend residence. The center of the U-shaped building is the main living area; one wing contains the kitchen and bath area and the other serves as a special purpose room.

CREDITS
NAME & LOCATION: Weekend Residence, Oyster Bay Cove, New York
ARCHITECT: Peter Bentel, Bentel & Bentel Architects, Locust Valley, New York

Inside the building a large atrium was created to provide light to the interior of the apartments and to create a circulation system. The interior steel structural system was retained and used to support the skylight. Photographic credit: Bruce T. Martin.

CREDITS
NAME & LOCATION: San Marco/Lincoln Wharf, Boston, Massachusetts
ARCHITECT: Boston Architectural Team, Inc., Chelsea, Massachusetts
DEVELOPER: San Marco Housing Corporation, Boston, Massachusetts

Twenty North Michigan Avenue in Chicago, Illinois was originally built to house the operations of Montgomery Ward. It has been remodeled as modern office and retail space. Photographic credit: Hedrick-Blessing.

CREDITS
NAME & LOCATION: Twenty North Michigan Avenue Building, Chicago, Illinois
ARCHITECT: Nagle, Hartray & Associates, Ltd., Chicago, Illinois
DEVELOPER: U.S. Equities, Inc., Chicago, Illinois

The Hendley Building in Galveston, Texas was built in 1859 as cotton export offices. It is the last building on the row in the east end of the city's historic Strand area. A buttress system was devised to stabilize a badly deteriorated exposed party wall. Photographic credit: Taft Architects.

CREDITS
NAME & LOCATION: Hendley Building, Galveston, Texas
ARCHITECT: Taft Architects, Houston, Texas
DEVELOPER: Galveston Historical Foundation, Galveston, Texas

In its renovation, the curtain wall was revamped, different colored glass panels were used to highlight the structural bracing system of the building, and a new roof structure was added to provide definition.

CREDITS
NAME & LOCATION: Renaissance Tower, Dallas, Texas
ARCHITECT: Skidmore, Owings and Merrill, Chicago, Illinois
DEVELOPER: The Prudential Insurance Company of America

McAuley Hall, a 1920s college building, and an 1885 octagonal structure have been retained as part of the transformation of the campus. Photographic credit: RTKL Associates Inc. and Hedrick-Blessing.

CREDITS
NAME & LOCATION: USF&G Mount Washington Center, Baltimore, Maryland
ARCHITECT: RTKL Associates, Inc., Bernard J. Wulff, AIA, Principal in Charge, Baltimore, Maryland
DEVELOPER: United States Fidelity and Guaranty Company, Baltimore, Maryland

An expansion and new entrance to the Veterans' Administration Hospital in Sioux Falls, South Dakota uses the sloping topography of the site. The new parking area is screened from the main hospital facility. Photographic credit: Architectural Images.

CREDITS
NAME & LOCATION: Veterans' Administration Hospital Addition and Renovation, Sioux Falls, South Dakota
ARCHITECT: Spitznagel, Architects, Engineers, Planners, Sioux Falls, South Dakota

A large atrium, cut through the center of the building, is visible through the glass storefronts of the building. The atrium, festooned with bright colors, creates a visual attraction to draw people into Chinatown.

CREDITS
NAME & LOCATION: *China Trade Center, Boston, Massachusetts*
ARCHITECT: *Boston Architectural Team, Inc., Chelsea, Massachusetts*
DEVELOPER: *Chinese Economic Development Council, Boston, Massachusetts*

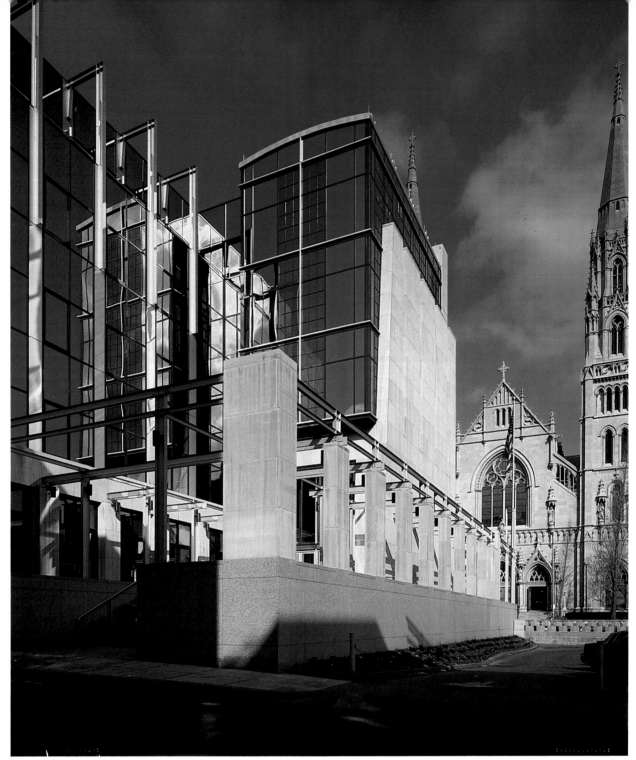

CREDITS
NAME & LOCATION: Software Engineering Institute, Pittsburgh, Pennsylvania
ARCHITECT: Joint venture of Bohlin Powell Larkin Cywinski and Burt Hill Kosar Rittelman
   Associates, Pittsburgh, Pennsylvania
STRUCTURAL ENGINEER: Dotter Engineering, Inc.
MECHANICAL ENGINEERS: Burt Hill Kosar Rittelman Associates, Pittsburgh, Pennsylvania
DEVELOPER: Regional Industrial Development Council of Southwestern Pennsylvania as
   developer for Carnegie Mellon University, Pittsburgh, Pennsylvania

**The Software Engineering Institute is on the campus of the Carnegie Mellon University
in Pittsburgh, Pennsylvania. There was no clear precedent for a building of this type in
an urban environment. The designers chose to respond to the surrounding
environment of university and civic architecture, which includes St. Paul's Cathedral.
Photographic credit: Karl A. Backus, Photography.**

CREDITS
NAME & LOCATION: Atlantic Coastline Building, Washington, D.C.
PRESERVATION ARCHITECT: Building Technology Conservation and Oehrlein and Associates, Washington, D.C.
DEVELOPER: Westminster Investing Corporation

The Atlantic Coastline Building in Washington, D.C. was originally built in 1892. As part of the revitalization program of the Pennsylvania Avenue Development Corporation, the building was carefully dismantled and its facade was rebuilt as part of a new office building development. Photographic credit: William Lebovich.

In New York City, late nineteenth-century fire and police stations, housed in two separate buildings, were combined using infill construction between and behind the existing structures. The infill portion of the project uses materials that match those of the original structures. Drawing credit: The Stein Partnership.

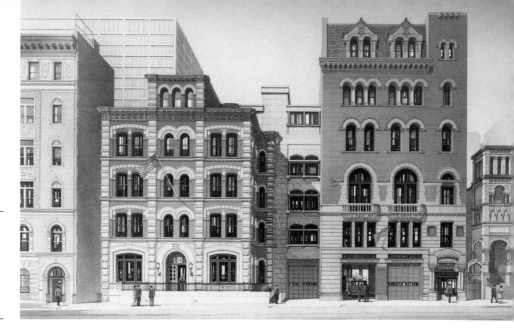

CREDITS
NAME & LOCATION: Combined Facility for 19th Precinct and Engine Co. 39 and Ladder Co. 16, New York, New York
ARCHITECT: The Stein Partnership, New York, New York
DEVELOPER: The City of New York

CREDITS
NAME & LOCATION: Sears House, Washington, D.C.
DESIGN ARCHITECT: Hartman-Cox Architects, Washington, D.C.
ARCHITECT: Geier Renfrow Brown (Phase I); Leo A. Daly (Phase II), Washington, D.C.
PRESERVATION ARCHITECT: John Milner Associates
DEVELOPER: Sears, Roebuck and Co., Washington, D.C.

As part of the redevelopment scheme for Pennsylvania Avenue in Washington, D.C., two historic buildings located adjacent to each other were slated for preservation. An infill structure between the two buildings, the twin turreted Apex Building and the former studio of Civil War photographer Mathew Brady, serves as the connecting link between the two structures and houses mechanical equipment, elevators, and fire stairs so that the historic buildings could be preserved. Photographic credit: Arnold Kramer.

The San Francisco Gift Center is housed in a historic concrete warehouse. The large building contains 300,000 square feet of space and a five-story central atrium. Photographic credit: Douglas Symes.

CREDITS
NAME & LOCATION: The Gift Center, San Francisco, California
ARCHITECT: Kaplan/McLauglin/Diaz, San Francisco, California

In Minneapolis, Minnesota, a former factory complex has been renovated as the International Market Square comprising 250 showrooms. A five-story glass-roofed atrium ties the complex together and provides stage areas for special events. Photographic credit: Balthazar Korab, Ltd.

CREDITS
NAME & LOCATION: International Market Square, Minneapolis, Minnesota
ARCHITECT: Kaplan/McLauglin/Diaz, San Francisco, California in association with
    Winsor/Faricy Architects

Underwear Factory to Showrooms

The former Munsingwear Factory in Minneapolis, Minnesota comprises four large brick buildings totally over 650,000 square feet of space. The complex, built between 1891 and 1912, has been renovated into 250 showrooms comprising the International Market Square. The various structures in the complex are tied together with a five-story, glass-roofed atrium of 19,000 square feet. The former boiler house has been converted into the entrance lobby for the complex. The atrium area with ironwork balconies and glass-enclosed elevators includes three stages and is designed for use as a special events facility.

Nineteenth-Century Downtown Building Reused as Retail Center

The Boylston Building, built as retail and office space in 1887, is located at the gateway of Chinatown in Boston, Massachusetts. The building is important historically and is listed on the National Register of Historic Places, as well as a designated Boston landmark. By the time the building was acquired by the Chinese Economic Development Council in 1978, it had been completely abandoned. The building has been revitalized as a central retail space leading into Chinatown with additional office space. To create a visual attraction for tourists visiting Boston's Chinatown, a large atrium was created in the center

A large atrium, cut through the center of the building, is visible through the glass storefronts of the building. The atrium, festooned with bright colors, creates a visual attraction to draw people into Chinatown.

The China Trade Center in Boston, Massachusetts is located in the historic Boylston Building built in 1887. Rehabilitated as a retail center with additional office space, the building stands at the entrance to Boston's Chinatown. Photographic credit: Bruce T. Martin.

CREDITS
NAME & LOCATION: China Trade Center, Boston, Massachusetts
ARCHITECT: Boston Architectural Team, Inc., Chelsea, Massachusetts
DEVELOPER: Chinese Economic Development Council, Boston, Massachusetts

of the building. The entire interior was gutted and rebuilt around the atrium, which is visible through a glass storefront covering two sides of the building.

To emphasize the building's association with Chinatown, bright primary colors and Chinese kites and paper dragons festoon the interior atrium. A brick plaza was built in front of the building, and a new pedestrian entrance was created. The first three floors of the building house retail space; office space for various businesses is located on the remaining three floors.

Because of the building's historic designation, special attention was paid to the restoration of the building's facade. The wooden storefronts of the original building have been restored and careful attention was given to the restoration of the windows. The original configuration of the windows was retained, and each one was rebuilt to accommodate new double-paned thermal glazing to replace the original single-paned glazing.

Medical Building Transformed into Hotel

The Medical Arts Building was originally built in 1926 in downtown San Antonio, Texas next door to the Alamo. Designed in a neo-Gothic style, the building sits on a triangular-shaped lot and contains 130,000 square feet on 12 floors. Listed on the National Register of Historic Places, the building has been remodeled three times, in 1940, 1950, and 1970; during these modernizations, virtually all of the elaborate interior finishes had been destroyed. One of the few features of the original interior that survived was the marble wainscoting in the lobby, which was saved and reused.

The rest of the interior was gutted to create the building's new use as a luxury hotel. Each room is approximately 350 square feet and has luxurious finishes and furnishings. Room furnishing costs averaged $4,000 to $6,000 per room compared with a hotel industry standard of between $1,000 and $1,200 per room. Bathrooms are designed to be extensions of the hotel rooms and incorporate sliding glass and wood "shoji" screens.

In San Antonio, Texas, a former medical building designed in a distinctive neo-Gothic style has been remodeled into the luxury Emily Morgan Hotel. Photographic credit: HOK Photography.

CREDITS
NAME & LOCATION: The Emily Morgan Hotel, San Antonio, Texas
ARCHITECT: Hellmuth, Obata & Kassabaum, Inc., St. Louis, Missouri
DEVELOPER: Integrand, San Fransisco, California

High School Becomes Office Building

The first high school in Oklahoma—Central High School in Oklahoma City—was built in 1909. The building combined the Beaux-Arts style with Gothic revival and is listed on the National Register of Historic Places. The building had been abandoned for several years and was littered with debris and covered with graffiti by the time it was being considered for renovation for new offices for Southwestern Bell.

CREDITS
NAME & LOCATION: One Bell Central, Oklahoma City, Oklahoma
ARCHITECT/ENGINEER: HTB, Inc., Oklahoma City, Oklahoma
DEVELOPER: Southwestern Bell Telephone Co., Oklahoma City, Oklahoma

The former Central High School in Oklahoma City, Oklahoma has been renovated for the corporate headquarters of Southwestern Bell. Photographic credit: R. Greg Hursley, Inc.

A central work area for the corporate operations of Southwestern Bell has been created in the former high school auditorium. The significant decorative features of the arch and balcony have been preserved. Photographic credit: R. Greg Hursley, Inc.

The major features of the interior that could be saved were the proscenium arch and balcony in the former school auditorium and the entrance into the library. The auditorium became a central court and major workspace. Glass panels and brass rails surround the former auditorium balcony and provide unobstructed views into this central workspace. A central skylight was rediscovered and reopened to provide light for interior work spaces. Other skylights were added in former utility wells and provide 25 percent of the total light in the building. The full 12-foot height of the original ceilings was retained. The former high school contains a little over 170,000 square feet of space including a museum of Central High memorabilia including trophies, period uniforms, and photographs in the original lobby and entry.

The Guaranty Building (also known as the Prudential Building) in Buffalo, New York is an important building in the history of American architecture. The building, designed by Adler and Sullivan in 1895, is one of the pioneering works in the development of the American skyscraper. By the late 1970s, the building had deteriorated badly and was threatened with demolition. A major effort was undertaken to rehabilitate the building. Photographic credit: Patricia Layman Bazelon.

CREDITS
NAME & LOCATION: *Guaranty Building (also known as the Prudential Building), Buffalo, New York*
ARCHITECT: *Cannon, Inc., Peter T. Flynn, Project Architect, Buffalo, New York*
DEVELOPER: *The Jeffersonian Corp., Cleveland, Ohio*

Restoring a Historic Skyscraper

One of the most important buildings in American architecture is Adler and Sullivan's 1895 Guaranty Building in downtown Buffalo, New York. New York's Senator Daniel Patrick Moynihan, an advocate of historic preservation, told a story about first seeing the building: "It was at a campaign meeting [in 1976], and I felt I had to get outside. I went for a walk and turned a corner two blocks away and there it was—'My God,' I said, 'there it is, the last Sullivan skyscraper!' I mean, it is our equivalent of the first Greek temple, the first Gothic cathedral."[1]

Senator Moynihan's appreciation of the landmark is well deserved. The Guaranty Building is a pioneering work in the development of the American skyscraper and is covered in rich and elaborate terra cotta ornamentation. The building has 13 floors and contains approximately 140,000 square feet of space.

By 1977 the once proud building had suffered through a series of remodelings and a fire that closed most of the interior. The owners soon applied for a demolition permit. A task force, established to recommend how the building could be saved, proposed that the interior of the first two floors be restored, that the exterior be cleaned, and that additional space be created by filling

[1] Benjamin Forgey, "The View from the Senator's Hill," *The Washington Post*, March 18, 1989, p. D1.

Prior to the restoration effort, Adler and Sullivan's ornate lobby had been almost completely obscured by a dropped ceiling and thoughtless response to fire code requirements. Photographic credit: Patricia Layman Bazelon.

in a light court. The restoration of the building, while admittedly costly, was greatly helped by the rehabilitation tax credits that were available when the work was undertaken.

The restoration of the first two floors involved both interior and exterior work. Adler and Sullivan's richly ornamented projecting storefronts had been removed in the 1950s and replaced by aluminum and glass storefronts placed behind the columns. The new projecting storefronts are replicated on the exterior, but are unornamented on the interior.

The main lobby of the building had been richly embellished with elaborate elevator cages, a marble mosaic frieze, an art glass ceiling, and a monumental stairway. It was virtually obscured through dropped ceilings and clumsy efforts to comply with fire safety code requirements. In the restoration, the elevator grillage was restored by using a wire-glass lining and a sprinkler system to satisfy code requirements. The main staircase together with its treads, balusters, column covers, and mid-point landing were restored to their original condition. The marble mosaic around the lobby was repaired where it had been damaged by the hung ceiling using marble salvaged from behind the elevator shafts. The upper floors meet modern office needs and reflect the original purpose of the building's construction: a speculative office building.

After restoration, the lobby was returned to what was intended by Adler and Sullivan. The staircase's treads, balusters, and column covers were restored to their original condition. The marble mosaic cornice in the lobby was repaired using salvaged marble. Photographic credit: Patricia Layman Bazelon.

Post Office Reused as Offices; Festival Market Place Added

The Old Post Office in Washington, D.C. occupies a strategic location on Pennsylvania Avenue midway between the Capitol and the White House. The building was completed in 1899 and from the 1930s until its restoration was constantly threatened with demolition because it did not conform to the architectural designs of the Federal Triangle that surrounds the building.

With its soaring clocktower, the Old Post Office was originally built as the headquarters for the U.S. Postal Service and the main post office for the city of Washington. A major feature of the interior is a central cortile or atrium

The Old Post Office in Washington, D.C. was originally built as the headquarters for the U.S. Postal Service in 1899. Today, the building is home to a number of Federal cultural agencies, including the National Endowment for the Arts, and a festival marketplace. Photographic credit: Peter H. Smith.

CREDITS
NAME & LOCATION: Old Post Office, Washington, D.C.
ARCHITECT: Arthur Cotton Moore, FAIA, Washington, D.C.
ARCHITECT FOR FESTIVAL MARKET PLACE: Benjamin Thompson, FAIA, Boston, Massachusetts.
DEVELOPER: General Services Administration, Washington, D.C.
DEVELOPER FOR THE PAVILION AT THE OLD POST OFFICE: The Evans Development Co., Washington, D.C.

The festival market place was created in the atrium of the building and includes three levels of shops and eateries. The framing members of a former skylight were retained as part of the design. Photographic credit: Peter H. Smith.

through the center of the building. The reuse program for the interior of the building included the refurbishment of the office space on the upper floors for continued use by the federal government. (The building is now home to a number of federal cultural agencies including the National Endowment for the Arts, the National Endowment for the Humanities, and the Institute for Museum Services.)

A festival market place was created in the lower section of the building. The main level was cut away to provide access to the basement level, which was reclaimed to become a food hall. A mezzanine level was added above the main floor to provide additional space for restaurants. A performance area on the lowest level reinforces the Old Post Office's ties to the arts.

The building does a lively business with tourists because it is located only blocks from the Mall and the downtown business area of the city. The tower is the second highest structure in the city after the Washington Monument and is operated as a sightseeing attraction by the National Park Service.

Train Station Preserved in Country's Largest Preservation Project

When it was completed in 1894, the Union Station in St. Louis, Missouri was the largest train station in the country. The work of Theodore C. Link of St. Louis, who won a national invited design competition in 1891 for the design of the facility, the station was intended to serve as the connecting link for train service between the east and west coasts. From the turn of the century until shortly after World War II, the station was the busiest in the nation with upward of 100,000 passengers using the station daily.

With the decline in cross-country train travel, Union Station also declined. In 1978 the station was closed for train operations. The station is listed on the National Register of Historic Places and is a designated Civil Engineering Landmark. In the nation's largest preservation reuse project, Union Station has been transformed into a new city within a city.

The station contains three main areas—the headhouse, the midway, and the train shed. The train shed is 606 feet by 810 feet with arches as high as 140 feet and covers over 11 acres. The total site covers 61.5 acres near the edge of St. Louis' central business district. The reuse scheme for Union Station has two major components—a retail center with a covered mall that includes

CREDITS
NAME & LOCATION: St. Louis Union Station, St. Louis, Missouri
ARCHITECT: Hellmuth, Obata & Kassabaum, Inc., St. Louis, Missouri
DEVELOPER: The Rouse Company

Union Station in St. Louis, Missouri has been preserved in the country's largest preservation project. The immense station, which was completed in 1894, covers over 11 acres and includes 825,000 square feet of space. The reuse project has two major components—a retail center with a covered mall called the Trainshed, which includes restaurants and shops, and a luxury hotel. Photographic credit: HOK Photography.

The original station's dining room has been restored to the designs of the original architect and is once again a centerpiece of Union Station. Photographic credit: HOK Photography.

shops, restaurants, and a luxury hotel. The total project includes 825,000 square feet of space.

The headhouse has been restored to the original Link design and includes the restoration of the famed Fred Harvey Restaurant, a hallmark of western train stations. Restoration also included original retail spaces in the station, 70 hotel rooms that were part of the original Terminal Hotel, and the public areas of the building.

The midway, originally the connecting point between the headhouse and the trains, continues to serve as the transition between the headhouse and the retail activities in the train shed. In addition to a new 550-room hotel, the train shed houses 160,000 square feet of shops and food facilities, and a one-acre lake that separates the parking area for over 2,000 automobiles from the main retail area.

CONSTRUCTING
ANEW AMID OLD

Robert Campbell, the architectural critic of the *Boston Globe*, succinctly explained this section's title when he wrote: "To build a new building in [a] homogeneous place . . . without copying or disrupting, is an architectural challenge."[1] Contextualism is an approach to design that makes a conscious effort to understand how a new structure will fit into an existing built environment and has been a major force in architectural design for a number of years. The popularity and forcefulness of the historic preservation movement in this country during the last quarter century have been significant factors in fostering a conscious contextual approach in architectural design. The popularity of postmodern design can be viewed as an effort to imbue new designs with the historical elements that connote contextualism on a broad scale—respect for historical antecedents of the American architectural vocabulary.

The importance of contextual architecture goes well beyond aesthetic considerations. In many areas of the country, there are historical, geographical, and climatological reasons why buildings are designed the way they are, and a good designer will pay attention to these factors. For example, steeply pitched roofs in New England serve the practical purpose of shedding snow. The large porches for which houses in the South are so well known derive from environmental factors. The overhanging porch provides shade and helps keep the interior of a house cool.

Contextualism in architecture is not meant to imply duplication of the existing buildings, but rather to provide a means of assessing the elements that contribute to a distinctive style or regional form of architecture. Contextual architecture attempts to use, not copy, historical antecedents.

Good contextual architecture should not create sameness. Rampant replication in the name of preserving the existing design motif of an area or historic

[1] Robert Campbell, "The Beauty-and-Beast Syndrome," *Boston Globe*, January 29, 1989, p. A14.

district can be carried too far. For example, the historic district in Alexandria, Virginia has an extraordinarily rich Colonial heritage and, in fact, was George Washington's hometown. A large number of residential and commercial buildings survive from the late eighteenth and early nineteenth centuries. A historic district, located in a section of the city called Old Town near the Potomac River, has been established to protect this architectural heritage. The strong preference of the historic district review board for colonial architecture has resulted in imitative new architecture that blurs the visual distinction of the growth of the city. In a sense, new buildings in Alexandria are forced into an old mold, which may not always be appropriate to the functional requirements of today's building needs.

For the designer to develop an appropriate contextual response is not an easy task. It is one that requires visual awareness, sensitivity, study, and thought.

Freestanding Construction in Old Neighborhoods

Freestanding construction amid existing structures is distinguished from additions, alterations, and other attached construction by the absence of any physical or functional connection between the new construction and adjacent buildings. The design and construction of a new building amid existing older or historic buildings present a range of challenges significantly different than those found in building addition designs. Some of the challenges involve the design elements of height, massing, scale, entrances, and materials. Building constraints imposed by zoning, use requirements, and, in some instances, historic preservation requirements can also present significant challenges.

Freestanding new construction has a number of advantages over building addition designs, the principal advantage being a designer's ability to meet precisely the requirements of the user, rather than compromising on certain needs and uses by adapting spaces in existing buildings. New building technologies, including HVAC and electronic/telecommunications equipment, can be incorporated more easily in a new building. Accessibility needs and circulation patterns can be accommodated with greater ease.

That a new building in an existing neighborhood takes its design cues from the surrounding buildings is often not a matter of choice, but required by zoning codes as well as design review boards. By proscribing permitted sizes and uses, zoning codes are in large measure responsible for determining the type of building that can be built in a given area. Similarly, building codes may limit the choice of material that can be used, depending on the building type.

In today's building process, boards such as neighborhood governments and historic design review boards often play extremely powerful and important roles in determining the look of a new building. Historic design review boards often have the power to determine whether a project will go forward or not and, in many instances, can extract sizable compromises from developers and designers.

Even without such constraints, designers often consider the context in which the new building will be situated. Tracy Kidder, writing about the design of a new single family house in the countryside, explains that a "building should fit its surroundings, both land around it and other buildings nearby. . . . The contextualist [architect] wants to capture some of the spirit of old buildings in new designs."[2] In this instance, there were no legal constraints of style or other requirements that would determine the form, design, and character of the new building. It was the determination of the designer and the client that such a house would be the most appropriate form and respect the existing heritage of the area.

A recent invited design competition for a new building on Capitol Hill in Washington, D.C. made use of a similar design philosophy. The new building for the federal judiciary is to be located next to Daniel Burnham's magnificent Union Station, just a few blocks from the U.S. Capitol. In explaining the goals of the competition, George White, the Architect of the Capitol, said that the new building should "not necessarily make a statement of its own but not spoil what was there, or perhaps a little of each."[3]

New Bank Building in Historic District

Near the entrance to the Georgetown section of Washington, D.C. a new 16,000-square foot building for a local bank is a conscious example of using the elements of the historic context as the basis for the design of a new building. The massing of the building reflects the streetscape of the main thoroughfare on which it is situated and uses traditional wall and window treatments. The entrance to the bank is created by separating the front wall from the mass behind. This opening is defined by a classical column and a fragment of an entablature that matches the facade of the adjacent theatre. In addition to the banking functions, the building includes office space, five apartments, and underground parking.

New Bank Building Restores Town Focus

During its heyday, Peterborough, New Hampshire was the real-life setting for Thornton Wilder's play, "Our Town." But by the late 1960s demolition of visually important buildings and replacement with parking lots had destroyed much of the character of the town. Particularly significant losses took place at the main intersection of the town where two old buildings were demolished.

One of the replacement buildings was a neo-Georgian local savings bank. By the late 1980s, the bank needed additional space and, through an imaginative design competition among local architects, sought to develop a new facility that could become the visual focus for the community. The new 20,000-square foot building uses native New Hampshire building materials in a design vocabulary that reflects the rich diversity of architecture in the community. The building is organized around a central circulation core that brings customers

---

[2] Tracy Kidder, *House*, New York: Avon Books, 1986, p. 52.
[3] Benjamin Forgey, "The Congressional Compromise," *The Washington Post*, February 4, 1989, p. G9.

A new bank building in the Georgetown section of Washington, D.C. makes use of architectural elements of the historic context to create a thoroughly modern building. The massing of the building reflects the prevailing scale of the streetscape; brick is the most common building material found in the historic district, and the classical column and entablature relate to architectural ornamentation on nearby buildings.
Photographic credit: Harlan Hambright & Associates.

CREDITS
NAME & LOCATION: Madison National Bank Building, Washington, D.C.
ARCHITECT: Martin & Jones, Washington, D.C.

The addition to the Peterborough Savings Bank in Peterborough, New Hampshire reflects the architectual diversity of the town. Photographic credit: Rob Karosis.

CREDITS
NAME & LOCATION: Peterborough Savings Bank, Peterborough, New Hampshire
ARCHITECT: Richard M. Monahon, Jr., AIA, Peterborough, New Hampshire

The new Peterborough Savings Bank restores the town focus by creating a new visual focus for the termination of the town's main street. Photographic credit: Richard M. Monahon, Jr., AIA.

New Structures Amid the Old

Two bridges and a clocktower show that awareness of an older context is not limited to buildings. On the campus of Stanford University in Palo Alto, California stands a clocktower that houses the original 1901 clockworks and bells that sat atop the Stanford Memorial Church until the earthquake of 1906 destroyed the church's steeple. In 1983 devoted faculty and students restored the works to prime condition and funds were raised to build a clocktower. The structure uses materials that blend with the Mission-style architecture of Stanford. Its scale is low, similar to its deceptively massed neighbors. It is distinctively contemporary with its flat roof and rectangular openings, yet it complements the Stanford campus in a historic and pleasing way.

Across the country in downtown Manhattan, a footbridge spans a busy street to link Trinity Church with its parish house. The new iron and steel bridge takes its cue from the wrought-iron fence around the Gothic revival church. The 85-foot-long bridge stands 16 feet above the ground and uses an arched Vierendeel truss that adds to its unencumbered appearance. The project received the 1989 Prize Bridge Award from the American Institute of Steel Construction.

A historic and strategic bridge that crosses the Delaware River between New York and Pennsylvania originally served as an aqueduct and later a vehicular toll bridge. Built in 1847, it was closed in 1977 because of a partial roadway collapse. Three years later, the bridge, designed by John A. Roebling, designer of the Brooklyn Bridge, was acquired by the National Park Service because of its historic importance as the oldest rope/wire suspension bridge in the country. By 1987 the bridge was returned to alternating one-way vehicular and pedestrian travel, but within the strict guidelines of historic preservation. A 9-inch concrete roadbed was laid over the aqueduct, but it is not visible from the riverbank because of the restored wooden superstructure. Grade-separated walkways protect pedestrians and serve to hide communications and power lines. In the event that a modern bridge is built nearby, the design of the Delaware Aqueduct is reversable and can revert to uses other than for vehicles. The project received a 1989 Honor Award from the American Institute of Architects.

The clocktower at Stanford University in Palo Alto, California, houses the original 1901 university clock. Its original home, in a church steeple, was destroyed by the 1906 earthquake. This 1983 structure uses materials and scale to blend in with the historic Stanford campus. Photographic credit: Peter H. Smeallie.

A new pedestrian bridge links Trinity Church with its parish house over a busy New York City street. The bridge was installed in a matter of hours as one piece using a single span configuration. Photographic credit: Peter Freed.

CREDITS
NAME & LOCATION: Trinity Church Pedestrian Overpass
ARCHITECT: Lee Harris Pomeroy Associates, New York, New York
ENGINEER: Amman & Whitney Consulting Engineers, New York, New York

CREDITS
NAME & LOCATION: Delaware Aqueduct, Minisink, New York/Lackawaxen, Pennsylvania
ARCHITECT: Beyer Blinder Belle, New York, New York
ENGINEER OF RECORD: Amman & Whitney, Edward Cohen, partner, New York, New York
OWNER: National Park Service, Mid Atlantic Regional Office, Philadelphia, Pennsylvania

The historic Delaware Aqueduct bridge over the Delaware River between Minisink, New York and Lackawaxen, Pennsylvania partially collapsed in 1977. The bridge's rebuilding maintained the historic cable and timber truss structure while providing contemporary use as a one-way vehicular bridge. Photographic credit: Alan Schindler.

into the bank from screened parking lots on two levels. It is fully accessible, and elevators provide circulation to all floors. The new building is connected to the original bank building via a covered walkway over the main driveway.

New Church Parish Hall

In Peterborough, New Hampshire, All Saints Church, built in 1923, needed more space to carry out church-related activities, including Sunday school, gatherings, weddings, and a second-hand shop. The decision was made to build a new parish hall across the street from the main church and rectory. The new structure was designed in a manner that used architectural idioms from the church building as well as the surrounding residential area. The new parish hall, which overlooks a nearby river, is clearly of modern vintage and very much an independent building on the site. At the same time, the building respects the historical antecedents of the town and the congregation.

The new Parish Hall at All Saints Church in Peterborough, New Hampshire uses architectural elements from the church building as well as nearby residential areas. Photographic credit: Duffy Monahon.

CREDITS
NAME & LOCATION: All Saints
   Church, Peterborough, New
   Hampshire
ARCHITECT: Richard M. Monahon,
   Jr., AIA, Peterborough, New
   Hampshire

At the University of Michigan in Ann Arbor, the new Alumni Center makes use of the predominant building materials of the campus—brick and limestone—to create a contemporary building that is part of the traditional campus. Photographic credit: Balthazar Korab, Ltd.

CREDITS
NAME & LOCATION: Alumni Center, University of Michigan, Ann Arbor
ARCHITECT: Hugh Newell Jacobsen, FAIA, Washington, D.C.

New College Alumni Center

The Alumni Center is an integral addition to the traditional architectural style of the University of Michigan campus in Ann Arbor. The predominant building materials of the campus—brick and limestone—are evident in the new center. The building abstracts the central elements and themes of the campus architecture to create a building that is distinct, yet clearly a part of the institution.

The use of bold geometric banding in granite on the brick building echoes the material on nearby campus buildings, but in a manner that emphasizes the differences in the two materials. The roof line of the new building draws inspiration from the roof lines of surrounding campus buildings, then abstracts them with severe angles.

Software Building in a Hard Environment

The home of the Software Engineering Institute (SEI) is on the campus of Carnegie Mellon University in Pittsburgh, Pennsylvania. SEI is operated by the university under contract to the Department of Defense. The goal of SEI is the advancement of software, especially a generation of new software. The site chosen for the home of SEI is at the edge of the common boundary of the Carnegie Mellon University campus and the University of Pittsburgh. The SEI

The Software Engineering Institute is on the campus of the Carnegie Mellon University in Pittsburgh, Pennsylvania. There was no clear precedent for a building of this type in an urban environment. The designers chose to respond to the surrounding environment of university and civic architecture, which includes St. Paul's Cathedral. Photographic credit: Karl A. Backus, Photography.

CREDITS
NAME & LOCATION: Software Engineering Institute, Pittsburgh, Pennsylvania
ARCHITECT: Joint venture of Bohlin Powell Larkin Cywinski and Burt Hill Kosar Rittelman Associates, Pittsburgh, Pennsylvania
STRUCTURAL ENGINEER: Dotter Engineering, Inc.
MECHANICAL ENGINEERS: Burt Hill Kosar Rittelman Associates, Pittsburgh, Pennsylvania
DEVELOPER: Regional Industrial Development Council of Southwestern Pennsylvania as developer for Carnegie Mellon University, Pittsburgh, Pennsylvania

The building uses a glass curtain wall for much of its facade. The granite base, punctuated by windows, parallels the rhythm and scale of the nearby Mellon Institute. The semicircular entrance plaza is on axis with St. Paul's Cathedral. Photographic credit: Karl A. Backus, Photography.

site is in the midst of two urban college campuses in one of the most heavily industrialized cities in the United States.

There was virtually no precedent for a building of this use in such an environment. The models of other buildings that housed facilities to support the development of software are usually found in suburban office research parks in places such as California's Silicon Valley.

The facilities in the SEI building have to serve two not always complementary functions. First, the building has to function as a laboratory in which advances in software development can be pursued. Second, the structure has to function as a conventional office building. The building clearly has to be able to provide great flexibility to accommodate the mission and goals of SEI.

The architects for the project chose to respond to the existing environment, which includes many early twentieth-century university and civic buildings. Directly across the street is the Mellon Institute, built in the 1930s in the neoclassic style with massive doric columns. Opposite the SEI site is St. Paul's Cathedral. St. Paul's is one of the tallest buildings in the immediate vicinity and includes two spires providing the emphasis to the vertical character of the church. The symmetry of the building emphasizes the central axis of the nave. Also nearby is the Cathedral of Learning at the University of Pittsburgh, which was designed in an academic Gothic vocabulary popular in the 1920s and 1930s.

The SEI includes over 150,000 square feet on five floors and a 400-car parking garage. The size of the new facility allowed the architects to respond to the monumental scale of the surroundings. SEI's height matches that of the adjacent Mellon Institute, and the bottom of the pediment of the Mellon Institute is echoed in a break in the curtain wall grid at the top of the SEI building.

The SEI employs a glass curtain wall for much of its facade. This choice was dictated by a number of factors including economy, speed of construction, and the need to provide light for perimeter offices. The curtain wall is set on a granite base punctuated by vertical windows and capped by limestone at the first floor level. This base parallels the rhythm and scale of the Mellon Institute and creates a visual link.

The use of masonry at the lower level of the SEI also responds to the predominant building material of the facades of other nearby buildings. The semicircular entry plaza for the SEI has entrances at either end and is on an axis with St..Paul's Cathedral so that it responds to the facade and orderliness of the monumental church. The principal entry into the SEI is a limestone entry pavilion, which is the tallest element of the SEI. The proportions of this entryway reflect the vertical spires of St. Paul's.

New Construction
Attached to
Old Buildings

With an emphasis today on reusing existing buildings, completely new construction is often attached to an existing structure to form a new, larger building. Similar to a building addition, the new construction and the original building are attached in some manner, but, unlike an addition, the new and the original function as independent entities. It is often the case that separate mechanical, electrical, and plumbing systems are maintained; however, in some manner, the structural systems of the new and original are often commingled.

Generally, the major distinction between a new attachment and an addition concerns the use of the new section. An addition is a new structure designed to support the functions carried out in the old building or vice versa. Attached new construction, as used in this chapter, can be independent of the existing building (although it does not necessarily have to be); there is no need to connect the old and the new since there is no complementary use. The old building and the new construction function as two independent structures and can be owned, developed, designed, and managed by entirely different entities.

Nevertheless, like Siamese twins, the two buildings are physically tied to one another, and there is some type of physical and design relationship between the two. For example, the original part of the building could continue to serve as offices, and an attached new tower could serve as a hotel. These two use types have many different requirements, especially for circulation patterns and periods of active use. As such, there is no need for the buildings to share building support systems, except, of course, in the case of joint structural considerations. In another case, the original building may serve as a lobby area for a hotel, while a new hotel tower is attached.

Another important distinction between attached new construction and additions is scale. In many instances, attachments to buildings are considerably larger

145

than the existing building on the site and can overshadow and literally surround what is there. For example, on the historic waterfront in the Georgetown section of Washington, D.C. there is a small row of eighteenth-century warehouses originally built to support the port functions of the area. In the late 1970s, a new office building was built that surrounds these historic structures on three sides. The eighteenth- and twentieth-century buildings are physically attached via a party wall, but they serve no common purpose. Nevertheless, the new structure was designed in a manner that does not detract from the historic character of the existing buildings. Examples such as this can be found throughout older sections of many American cities.

Whatever the nature of physical connection, a number of factors should be considered. The design contribution of the existing building should be carefully evaluated; the new structure should be designed to respect the architectural contribution of the existing building and its neighboring structures. Many of the considerations outlined in Section I on building additions are equally valid when developing a design approach for attaching a new building to an existing one.

Usually, new construction attached to an existing building is kept visually distinct. This can be accomplished in a number of ways, including a dramatic change in architectural style or varying the exterior materials between the original and the new. For example, an existing brick building may have a new building of precast concrete placed next to it. This change in materials will emphasize the difference between the two portions of a building.

If there is a structural connection between the two buildings, such connections should be carefully evaluated by qualified engineers to determine if interconnecting the two structures can be done in a safe and sound way. Many attached new buildings make use of a party wall, a retaining wall that is part of the building, or the foundations or footings of the building.

New construction occurs alongside older and, sometimes, historic structures because of a change in the economic character of an area and an accompanying change in the predominant use of the area (such as Georgetown's eighteenth-century waterfront changing from a warehouse district to a twentieth-century office and residential district). This change in use leads to changes in zoning to reflect the new economic realities. For example, an area that had been primarily a manufacturing and industrial area can become a part of the central business district of a city. In such instances, the existing warehouse and manufacturing facilities will become obsolete and will become mingled with new office building development and construction.

Expansion of Power Company Headquarters Building

The original headquarters building of the Alabama Power Company in Birmingham, Alabama was built in 1925 as a freestanding art deco-style building. A major addition was added to the building in 1955. Thirty years later, the power company needed still more room. The 1955 addition had an aluminum-clad curtain wall facade. As part of the project, the facade of this section of the complex was replaced with a new curtain wall of ceramic tile inlaid in precast concrete to match the color of the brick in the original section. The 1980s section consisted of a new 18-story office tower and a major atrium housing a 600-seat cafeteria and the lobby. The new building uses both a change in scale and materials to emphasize its separateness from the original building.

Although the buildings are interconnected and share the same use, each

The original headquarters of the Alabama Power Company in Birmingham was built in 1925 in an art deco style. In 1955 an aluminum curtain wall addition was added to the original structure

CREDITS
NAME & LOCATION: Alabama Power Company Headquarters, Birmingham, Alabama
ARCHITECT: Geddes Brecher Qualls Cunningham Architects, Philadelphia, Pennsylvania

The headquarters of the Alabama Power Company has been greatly expanded by attaching an 18-story office tower and central atrium space with a 600 seat cafeteria to the original part of the complex. The facade of the 1955 addition was replaced with a new curtain wall of ceramic tile inlaid in precast concrete to more closely match the original art deco building. Photographic credit: Jack Horner.

is a visually distinct building. The attached new construction graphically portrays growth and sense of power by preserving the visual impact of the original, highly ornamented art deco portion.

New Office Towers over Victorian Townhouses

Somehow the 1700 block of N Street, N.W., in Washington, D.C., a small street of charming Victorian era townhouses just a block south of DuPont Circle, survived amid a giant office construction boom in the Washington midtown area during the 1970s. The area in the rear of the townhouses had included, when built, a generous lot for stable and carriage houses as well as an alley to allow access to these facilities. This area provided sufficient space in which to construct a new office tower behind four of the historic townhouses.

The new office space is designed to relate both to the scale and design of Victorian townhouses as well as nearby speculative office buildings. However,

1752 N Street, N.W., in Washington, D.C., is the address of a new office development that includes the rehabilitation of four historic nineteenth-century townhouses together with a new office structure built behind the existing buildings. Photographic credit: Harlan Hambright & Associates.

CREDITS
NAME & LOCATION: 1752 N Street, N.W., Washington, D.C.
ARCHITECT: Martin & Jones, Washington, D.C.
DEVELOPER: Willco Construction Company, Rockville, Maryland

the skin of the curtain wall of the new office building is sheathed in brick so that it forms a link to the Victorian townhouses onto which it faces. A glass-enclosed courtyard separates the new offices from the townhouses and serves as the lobby for the new building. The courtyard also provides light for both. A horizontal band on the office tower establishes the height of the townhouses. The townhouses have served as office space and continue to do so. Entry to the new office space is gained by walking through the townhouses to a bank of elevators that is shared by both the existing building and the new office structure.

The new office structure relates to both the historic Victorian townhouses as well as nearby speculative office buildings. A metal band on the new office portion of the development outlines the rooflines of the townhouses. Photographic credit: Harlan Hambright & Associates.

New Parking Structure for Apartment Rehabilitation Project

In Pittsburgh, Pennsylvania a school building listed on the National Register of Historic Places has been rehabilitated into a desirable 77-unit apartment complex. The four-story school house features a stone course on the ground floor with brick above. Because parking presented an important amenity for the project, a new parking garage was constructed adjacent to the apartment complex. The new two-story parking garage is designed to mimic the stone coursing as well as the rhythm of the window openings and the planes of the facade on the main floor of the rehabilitated school building. The new garage building, although completely separate from the apartment complex, nevertheless uses design elements of the existing building in new ways to create a completely new building.

The rehabilitation of an old school in Pittsburgh, Pennsylvania as an apartment complex required new tenant parking. The new parking garage uses design elements of the existing school building to visually tie the two structures together.

CREDITS
NAME & LOCATION: The School
    House, Pittsburgh, Pennsylvania
ARCHITECT: The Rothschild
    Company/Architects,
    Philadelphia, Pennsylvania
DEVELOPER: Historic Landmarks for
    Living, Inc., Philadelphia,
    Pennsylvania

1880s Commercial Building and Its New Neighbor

Charles Pierre L'Enfant's eighteenth-century Baroque city plan for Washington, D.C., which created the core of the monumental capital city, resulted in many odd-angled streets. As the city grew, builders and designers attempted to cope with the intersections of these angled streets with varying degrees of success. At the intersection of Connecticut Avenue, Rhode Island Avenue, and M Street stands the Demonet Building. Built in 1880, the brick building uses a domed six-story and six-sided bay to address the odd angles that the streets create.

A few years ago, the building was threatened with demolition by a local developer. Local preservationists were able to save the building, and another more sympathetic development team found a way to highlight the Demonet Building by combining it with new construction. Today, the building houses the Washington branch of Burberry's.

The new construction, which makes full use of the allowable height and density permitted by zoning, rises 12 stories behind the historic building in a stepped design. The dome of the Demonet Building is highlighted by a large arched window that faces the odd intersection at the same angle as the prominent bay of the historic building. The new construction is a modern office tower with a precast stone facade. The cornice of the new building echoes the detailed dentilling of the brick work on the cornice of the Demonet Building. The new structure is entirely separate from the historic building, and the entrance to the new space is around the corner from the center axis of the project.

The 1880 Demonet Building in Washington, D.C. was combined with new construction to create a large office and retail complex. The design of the new office component echoes and reinforces the dominant architectural elements of the Demonet Building. Photographic credit: Peter H. Smith.

CREDITS
NAME & LOCATION: Demonet
   Building, Washington, D.C.
ARCHITECT: Skidmore, Owings &
   Merrill, Washington, D.C.
DEVELOPER: Second British
   American Properties, Inc.
   and Viking Property Group,
   Washington, D.C.

Large Project Combines Old with New

M Street in northwest Washington, D.C. is the site of another project that combines old buildings with new construction. There, two nineteenth-century school buildings were saved by the local school board. A developer–architect competition sponsored by the school board resulted in the scheme that combined the historic buildings with a new office building and associated open space.

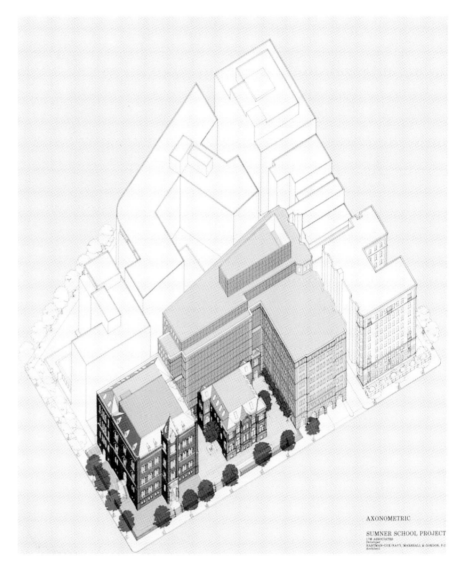

AXONOMETRIC

SUMNER SCHOOL PROJECT

Sumner Square in Washington, D.C. combines the rehabilitation of a historically important 1872 school building—the Sumner School—with the reconstruction of an 1880s school—the Magruder School—together with a large office, retail and commercial building set back to the rear of the school buildings. The project also contains two courtyards for pedestrians. Drawing credit: Hartman-Cox Architects.

CREDITS
NAME & LOCATION: Sumner Square, Washington, D.C.
ARCHITECT: Hartman-Cox Architects, Washington, D.C./Navy, Marshall & Gordon Architects
DEVELOPER: Boston Properties with the D.C. School Board

Two nineteenth-century school buildings form the heart of an urban design project that combines the old buildings with new office space in the rear and to one side. Photographic credit: Peter H. Smith.

The project has won high praise. The Sumner School, prominently sited at the corner of 17th and M Streets, was built in 1872 and was designed by Adolph Cluss, a prominent architect of many public buildings in post-Civil War Washington. The Magruder School is located in the middle of the block. Built in the 1880s, and a less pretentious building than the Sumner School, it nevertheless is an excellent example of the red brick Victorian school building. The eastern end of the block, at 16th Street, is occupied by the historic Jefferson Hotel, built in 1923 and designed by Jean Henri de Sibour, an architect well known for many Beaux-Arts buildings throughout monumental Washington.

The centerpiece of the project is the reuse of the Sumner School. The building's Victorian Gothic tower, polychromed tile roof, and hooded windows have been restored; it now serves as a museum for the public schools of Washington as well as hosting numerous social events.

The design was conceived as a complete urbanscape for the entire block. Because of the layout of Washington streets, the site was essentially trapezoidal. The three major elements that comprise the design are the restoration and rehabilitation of the two school buildings, the development of a new office complex behind and to the east of the school buildings, and development of open space between the schools and the office component.

The school buildings occupy the visual center of the composition. To achieve the desired result, the Magruder School was partially dismantled and shifted 8 feet to the west. Behind the school a curtain wall office building was developed and rises to the full height allowed by the zoning of the site. The configuration of the buildable area allowed the developer to intensively develop the block without impairing the visual prominence of the red brick school buildings. This section of the office building is located behind the Magruder School approximately 90 feet from the sidewalk and is sheathed in gray reflective glass. Two brick entrances to the office building flank the Magruder School and reflect the nineteenth-century buildings on the site.

Flagstone courtyards flank the Magruder School. The east end of the office building, which defines the boundary, reflects the height, style, color, and cornice of the adjacent Jefferson Hotel. The total composition shows how old and new architecture can be combined for different uses while creating an entirely pleasing and usable streetscape.

10 Retaining Facades

During the last decade a popular way of combining old and new architecture has been the preservation of only the facade or front of a building as part of an entirely new structure. Facade preservation is often viewed as an acceptable compromise when an entire building cannot be preserved.

Although this approach has been widely criticized, there are a number of reasons that facade preservation is practiced. Facades are retained to preserve the visual streetscape and maintain a sense of scale and a sense of place—if it's not the old, familiar building, at least it's the front of the old, familiar building. Facade retention is also a defensive tactic among preservationists. Mary Means, former vice-president of the National Trust for Historic Preservation, points out that preservationists sometimes settle for saving merely a facade "rather than risk the quality of design that is likely to replace it."[1]

The facade is often the most important element of a building, sometimes the only element that has received any design attention. For example, in a typical row house, the important exterior visual element is the front elevation. The side walls are built for structural purposes and are not meant to be visible. Similarly, rear elevations may not receive any design attention if they are not visible elements of the building composition.

In some cases, facades are saved because significant alterations to the interior and exterior of the building have occurred to such an extent that the facade is the only part of the original structure remaining. For example, an older building may have gone through so many changes in use with consequent substantial changes to the interior that the original spatial configuration is no longer discernible. In such instances, the facade of a building may be the only element of the structure that deserves preservation.

As a neighborhood changes from residential or small-scale commercial to

[1] Allen Freeman, "Old Facades Fronting for New Construction," *Architecture*, November 1983, p. 71.

a use that requires larger or taller buildings, it is often only the facades that survive the development activity, especially when the zoning requirements preclude the previous use of the original buildings. In such instances, it may not be economically feasible to attempt to retain the original use of a building, or the use may be precluded by current zoning ordinances. In Baltimore, Maryland, the Mayor announced in April 1989 that the facade of the historic Mercantile Safe Deposit and Trust Building would be rebuilt as part of a $90 million new tower complex; the facade was taken down piece by piece and each item was numbered and stored. The pieces will be cleaned and reassembled as part of the new tower.

Facade preservation ranges from keeping only the building materials that comprise the actual front of the building to retaining and reusing the front and portions of the side walls. Once the decision has been made to retain or preserve the facade of an older building, as much of the original should be used as possible. The literature is replete with ridiculed "facade compromises" in which just pieces of the facade are used or fake reproductions are built. In a number of instances, the facade is treated as a paste-on decorative element rather than as an integral part of a new project. For example, in Buffalo, New York, a portion of a historic facade has been preserved as a decorative element in front of the glass curtain wall of the office of the Goldome Bank for Savings Corporate Headquarters.

Facade preservation often involves complicated structural engineering. During the construction process, the facade can become a free wall with no lateral support. To maintain the facade in the original position until the remainder of the building can be completed, the wall must be stabilized. Steel beam buttresses are used to stabilize the wall and prevent its crumbling during the pounding and vibrations of construction. The facade is then tied to the new construction section by interweaving the structural system with the new building. The point at which the new construction meets the old facade is an important juncture that has to be carefully designed to create a smooth transition.

In Buffalo, New York, a portion of the facade of an existing building has been incorporated as a decorative element into the facade of a modern curtain wall office structure.

Facades on America's Main Street

1001 Pennsylvania Avenue is one of the premier projects along the revitalized Pennsylvania Avenue in the heart of Washington, D.C.'s downtown area. The project occupies a full city block and includes 795,000 square feet of office space and 44,000 square feet of retail space. The building rises to the full 14 floors allowed by Washington's zoning and height restrictions. When the site was first considered, there were five historic structures on three sides of the block.

1001 Pennsylvania Avenue is part of the revitalization of America's Main Street in Washington, D.C. The massive project includes the rehabilitated facades of historic buildings on three sides of the building, which occupies an entire city block. Photographic credit: Peter H. Smith.

CREDITS
NAME & LOCATION: 1001 Pennsylvania Avenue, Washington, D.C.
DESIGN ARCHITECT: Hartman-Cox Architects, Washington, D.C.
CONSTRUCTION DOCUMENTS: Smith, Segreti & Tepper, Washington, D.C.
PRESERVATION ARCHITECT: Oehrlein and Associates, Washington, D.C.
DEVELOPER: Cadillac-Fairview

The old facades not only break up the massing of the large project through differing setbacks and materials, but also provide pedestrian scale to the building's streetscape. Photographic credit: Peter H. Smith.

As the design developed, the historic structures provided the impetus. The building is massed toward the center of the site and steps back at intervals beginning with the existing historic buildings. The facades of the five historic structures—a brick moving company warehouse on 10th Street and four structures, including a former fire house, on 11th Street that wrap around the corner onto E street—have been restored and embedded into the overall composition of the project. The old facades provide pedestrian scale to the large project and break up the massing not only in the setbacks but also through use of differing materials and colors.

Building Reerected as Part of Redevelopment Project

The Atlantic Coastline Building, located in Washington, D.C. on a conspicuous corner of Pennsylvania Avenue between the Capitol and the White House, was constructed in 1892 for the Atlantic Coastline Company; it was designed by James G. Hill, a prominent late nineteenth-century Washington architect. Like many of Hill's buildings, the Atlantic Coastline Building uses rusticated stone in a strong composition. The odd angle created by the intersection of Washington's diagonal streets was used by Hill to advantage by creating a rounded corner facing west toward the Capitol.

In 1907 the upper floors of the building were remodeled when it underwent the first of a series of makeovers as various hotels, which lasted until 1942. It was then used by various agencies of the federal government until 1967. The building remained largely vacant until its preservation was undertaken in 1986.

The building is located in the Pennsylvania Avenue redevelopment area, which is overseen by a federal agency charged with revitalizing the historic downtown section of Washington. A major new office project was planned for the block on which the Atlantic Coastline Building was located. As part of the new project, the decision was made to save the facade of the historic structure. However, structural investigations revealed that the facade of the building could not be stabilized sufficiently to be maintained in place during the construction of the new office building.

The architects for the preservation work photogrammetrically recorded the building and prepared drawings of the existing historic facade. The building was then carefully dismantled by hand and stored until site conditions permitted the reerection of the facade as part of the overall project. When the building was reconstructed, its height and width were changed as well as the entrance for the structure to meet modern construction standards and the requirements of the new office building.

The Atlantic Coastline Building in Washington, D.C. was originally built in 1892. As part of the revitalization program of the Pennsylvania Avenue Development Corporation, the building was carefully dismantled and its facade was rebuilt as part of a new office building development. Photographic credit: William Lebovich.

CREDITS
NAME & LOCATION: Atlantic Coastline Building, Washington, D.C.
PRESERVATION ARCHITECT: Building Technology Conservation and Oehrlein and Associates, Washington, D.C.
DEVELOPER: Westminster Investing Corporation

The facades of two eighteenth-century buildings, which originally housed the operations of the federal government, have been restored and incorporated into a new office development at 1911 Pennsylvania Avenue in Washington, D.C. The development includes a major new building behind and around the historic townhouses. Photographic credit: Peter H. Smith.

CREDITS
NAME & LOCATION: 1911 Pennsylvania Avenue, N.W., Washington, D.C.
ARCHITECT: ICON, Peter Vercelli, Washington, D.C.

Parts of Eighteenth-Century Home of Federal Government Saved

In the nation's capital's early days, a group of seven townhouses on Pennsylvania Avenue, near the future site of the White House, served as the home of the government until more permanent and grander quarters were built. These buildings dating from 1793 were simply referred to as "The Seven." By the beginning of the 1980s, only portions of two of the buildings remained standing in the center of the block. The others had been demolished in the 1950s and 1970s to make way for modern office buildings. The two remaining structures had been extensively altered, the last use being as a popular Italian restaurant. However, the facades of the original two remained, although these small buildings were surrounded by modern office buildings.

When the site was considered for development, the various review boards in Washington approved a plan that retained the two facades and incorporated them into a new office project. The facades became part of reconstructed eighteenth-century townhouses that, in turn, were incorporated into a building that fills the space between two office projects at either end of the block.

The new building, although literally hovering over the historic townhouses, appears almost to be floating over them because glass is used extensively to create an airy feeling. The lobby for the new office building is adjacent to the townhouses and makes use of the rear of the buildings for an interior courtyard.

University Incorporates Old Buildings into New Speculative Office Venture

Red Lion Row is the vernacular name for a major project undertaken by George Washington University. The project encompasses more than half of a city block along Pennsylvania Avenue between the White House and historic Georgetown in Washington, D.C. George Washington University has developed a number of speculative office buildings on the perimeters of its in-town campus as a way of generating income.

CREDITS
NAME & LOCATION: 2000 Pennsylvania Avenue, N.W., Washington, D.C.
ARCHITECT: Hellmuth, Obata and Kassabaum, Washington, D.C. and John Carl Warnecke & Associates, Washington, D.C.
DEVELOPER: The George Washington University, Washington, D.C.

2000 Pennsylvania Avenue is a major project in Washington, D.C. that combines the preservation of elements of historic nineteenth-century row houses that existed on the site with a major new office building. The new office building does not attempt to use the stylistic elements of the townhouses, but rather is designed to be visually separate from the historic structures. Photographic credit: Peter H. Smith.

The project retained all salvageable parts of the historic townhouses. In some instances, the whole building is incorporated into the project; in others, portions of the existing walls were reused. In two cases only the facades of the buildings could be preserved. The space between the rear elevations of the historic townhouses and the new office building is a retail galleria. Photographic credit: Peter H. Smith.

The Red Lion Row project, called 2000 Pennsylvania Avenue by the university, includes nearly 400,000 square feet of office space as well as a large shopping galleria. The site of the project is on axis with the major campus quadrangle, and the university viewed it as an opportunity to develop not only an income-producing property, but a symbolic gateway to the campus as well. The site that was eventually assembled by the university in the late 1970s included a row of nineteenth-century townhouses in various states of disrepair.

The name Red Lion Row comes from a well-known tavern that had occupied one of the townhouses. The row had been declared historic by the city following a number of intense preservation controversies between the previous owner of a number of the rowhouses and the local preservation group, Don't Tear It Down. The university knew of the community interest in the preservation of the properties, and the initial plans developed by the university and their architects called for the preservation of little more than the facades of the townhouses.

The new office building for the university, as originally designed, had busy vertical elements that mimicked the width of the existing buildings. Neither aspect of the original scheme was acceptable to the preservation group nor the review boards that had to approve the project. The university, their architects, the preservation and community organizations, and the various review boards went through a number of different schemes and proposals to arrive at an approach that would be acceptable. The position of Don't Tear It Down and the neighborhood community groups was that more than merely the facades of the buildings were important and that the footprints of the existing structures should be saved. In the end, the scheme that was approved and built retained all salvageable portions of the nineteenth-century buildings.

The buildings are linked to the new structure by a skylighted galleria of retail stores, galleries, and restaurants. The new office building went through a number of designs, the idea being to create a background building that would complement the historic rowhouses.

With so many players involved in the design of the whole project, the result was criticized as being the one that displeased the fewest number of participants. The new office tower is a compromise to keep historic structures and the new office building visually separate. This was achieved, but the result is that the new office building overwhelms the historic row. All parties did get most of what they wanted from the project—George Washington University got its income-producing office building and the preservationists saved the townhouses—but in aesthetic terms the project ended up pleasing almost no one and has been the subject of intense criticism since it was constructed.

The first four floors of a 1911 Chicago skyscraper have been incorporated into a new building called Manufacturers Hanover Plaza. Photographic credit: Peter H. Smeallie.

CREDITS
NAME & LOCATION: *Manufacturers Hanover Plaza, Chicago, Illinois*
DESIGN ARCHITECT: *Moriyama & Teshima, Toronto, Ontario, Canada*
ASSOCIATE ARCHITECT: *Holabird and Root, Chicago, Illinois*
STRUCTURAL ENGINEER: *Cohen-Barreto-Marchertas, Inc.*
MECHANICAL/ELECTRICAL ENGINEERS: *Ammar Consulting Engineers*
DEVELOPER: *Fidinam (U.S.A.), Inc.*

The new building, a 37-story office tower, has an aluminum and glass curtain wall facade. The base of the curtain wall retains the original ornate terra cotta facade. Photographic credit: Wayne Cable.

Part of Chicago Skyscraper Saved in New Skyscraper

Manufacturers Hanover Plaza in Chicago occupies a prominent corner in Chicago's Loop. The new building is a 37-story office tower that includes slightly over 800,000 square feet of space. The project is one of the first in Chicago to include the retention of portions of the facade of the building that formerly occupied the site. The original building on the site had been a 16-story office building designed by Holabird & Roche in 1911.

In the new design, the first four floors of the original terra cotta and granite facade have been preserved and restored as part of the new office tower. The portion of the original building that had faced onto an alley and was constructed of plain brick was demolished along with the rest of the building as part of the overall project. The preserved facade maintains the existing streetscape in this area of Chicago's financial district. The ornate facade also provides a marked contrast to the blue aluminum and glass curtain wall building that rises behind it. The architects for the project were able to use most of the existing foundation caissons that had been sunk to bedrock in the structural system of the new building.

11

Site and Urban Design

Site and urban design considerations are important, but often overlooked, elements of the planning and execution of a project that involves combining old and new construction. As surely as bad design can influence one's attitude toward a building, insensitive attention to the site and surrounding area can color one's opinion of a neighborhood or an area. Site and urban design considerations involve a building's relationship to its physical surroundings including landscape architectural elements. A building's design relationship to adjacent buildings—how style, massing, height, and materials of the new building mix with the nearby buildings—is also a crucial consideration.

Site and urban design issues play a large role in determining the overall impact of a project, especially its reception by both building occupants and the community at large. Such considerations are amplified in crowded urban areas in which the need to provide light, air, and greenery is paramount.

Site and urban design considerations include topography, access, lighting, signage, plantings, views and vistas, security, public art, and street furniture. In some large-scale projects, designers have tried to provide natural environmental amenities on the interior through large, sunlight-filled indoor atria.

Where the landscape of a project is a significant design consideration, efforts to take advantage of the natural topography make good landscape preservation sense. By following the natural contours of the land, environmental damage can be minimized, and the new construction can be enhanced through its site design. For example, a new residential or office project in a scenic setting will be sited to take advantage of available views and vistas. Proximity to water, whether for views or for sound such as near a brook, is an attractive natural element and is often an integral element of site planning. Environmental and ecological regulations will determine, to some degree, the ability of new structures to make use of water as an integral element of building siting.

The natural setting can heavily influence the microclimate of a new building. Depending on the characteristics of the site, a building can experience substantial heat gain and loss. Blacktop parking lots surrounding a building will retain heat; leafy trees will keep a building cooler in summer and allow sunlight in winter. This information should be part of planning for the heating and cooling loads for the building.

Providing space for automobile parking is a constant and vexing issue in site and urban design. Although parking is mandatory for most new projects, parking requirements need to be balanced and weighed against the physical surroundings and architectural qualities of the project. Parking considerations must include attention to safety concerns. As much as possible, pedestrians and vehicles should be separated, and speed should be carefully controlled in parking areas.

As a general rule, parking should be screened from view. For example, with sufficient land, parking can be located behind the least important facade of a building. Similarly, driveways and approaches to the parking area can be screened through the use of plantings. The driveway can be depressed below the prevailing contour of the land, or it can be sited in such a way that it is not visually obtrusive. In some instances, the vehicular approach to a project is an important design element, and the driveway becomes a prominent feature of the overall composition. This is particularly true where a building has a long setback from a highway. For example, antebellum mansions in the South were consciously sited at the end of long drives, often flanked by large trees, to create a sense of drama and expectancy.

The relationship of a new building to transportation means other than the automobile is an important consideration. Access to subway systems, as well

Parking area surrounded by industrial buildings in Philadelphia, Pennsylvania, prior to conversion to apartments.

CREDITS
NAME & LOCATION: The Chocolate Works, Philadelphia, Pennsylvania
ARCHITECT: The Rothschild Company/Architects, Philadelphia, Pennsylvania
DEVELOPER: Historic Landmarks for Living, Inc.

as bus shelters for riders during inclement weather, are part of an overall site plan for a new urban building.

The ease of pedestrian access to a building should not be taken for granted. For example, without adequate and frequent signs with directions, maps, and place names, it is very easy for pedestrians to lose their way. In multiuse facilities, attention needs to be paid to defining clearly the intended entrance into the different parts of the building. For example, a recent conversion of an industrial structure to luxury apartments in Philadelphia, Pennsylvania made use of a parking area to create an attractive forecourt and entrance to the project. The entrance provides an articulated drive for automobiles along with pedestrian amenities. Means must be provided to ensure that provisions for access by the handicapped are included in the planning for the building.

The parking area has been remodeled as the forecourt and entrance to The Chocolate Works, a luxury apartment development. The entrance includes a landscaped circular drive.

Public access to open space is an important need for many urban dwellers as well as office tenants. The design of the space, whether it is a plaza, a meadow, or a courtyard, is critical to the overall perception of the entire project by the public and the building occupants.

Public art can be a part of the project. As Ronald Lee Fleming, an advocate for what he terms "lovable objects," wrote several years ago, these lovable objects "acknowledge popular culture as much as [they] recognize that many people find contemporary spaces barren and uninviting. It represents a growing reassessment of the modern movement—one taking place where people are most affected—on the city's ground floor."[1] Such art helps to define a sense of place and provide association.

Local governments understand the benefits of including public art as part of the site design program. In a number of towns and cities, developers are permitted zoning bonuses for the inclusion of public art in their projects. In Bethesda, Maryland, for example, developers are permitted to increase the size of their projects beyond that allowed under the zoning regulations by using public art projects as an integral part of the overall development.

What is generically referred to as street furniture should also be a part of a site design program. Street furniture refers to the benches, tables, chairs, and shelters that are used by people for leisure and recreation. Street furniture should allow people to rest, to enjoy the open air, to eat lunch, or converse in a relaxed atmosphere.

Lighting for safety, security, and as an art form has received a great deal of attention in the last few years. Adequate lighting for the land around a building, especially the parking lot, must be a part of the overall site design program. In a number of cities around the country, lighting a building at night to create a dramatic effect is popular. Perhaps the most famous example is the studied lighting of the art deco Chrysler Building in Manhattan. The lighting highlights the sculptural qualities of the building and makes it visible well beyond the confines of the city.

Landmark School Campus Revitalized

Tregaron, the one-time estate of William Davies, former U.S. Ambassador to the Soviet Union, is now the centerpiece of the Washington International School, located in the Cleveland Park section of Washington, D.C. A recent revitalization capitalized on the existing physical and architectural assets of the school to create new spaces for the students. An old greenhouse was converted into two new light and airy classrooms for the upper school and a new academic building was constructed. The design of the new academic building draws its inspiration from the Georgian Revival architecture of the landmark Tregaron Mansion, which is listed on the National Register of Historic Places.

The siting of the academic building was specifically designed to take advantage of the topography of the site and is located on the edge of a wooded ravine. In the next phase of development, the academic building will be joined by a new gymnasium, which will be similarly sited to take advantage of the hilly campus. The master plan includes new terraces and walkways throughout the campus, and a formal academic street defines the functions of the school.

[1] Ronald Lee Fleming, "Lovable Objects Challenge the Modern Movement," *Landscape Architecture*, Vol. 71, no. 1, January 1981, p. 89.

The master plan for the Washington International School in Washington, D.C. shows the academic street, a focal point around which the expansion of the campus is planned. The campus occupies a hilly site in the northwest section of the city. Drawing credit: Bowie-Gridley Architects.

CREDITS
NAME & LOCATION: The Washington International School, Washington, D.C.
ARCHITECT: Bowie-Gridley Architects, Washington, D.C.
ENGINEER: CAD-CON, Inc.

FUTURE GYMNASIUM

EXISTING CARRIAGE HOUSE

NEW ACADEMIC BUILDING

ACADEMIC STREET

EXISTING COTTAGE

EXISTING CLASSROOM BUILDING

EXISTING DACHA

MANSION

Washington International School
MASTER PLAN

This former greenhouse, which had originally been part of Ambassador Joseph Davies' estate, has been converted into light and airy classroom space. Photographic credit: Maxwell Mackenzie.

The new academic building on the school campus overlooks a wooded ravine. The design of the academic building is drawn from the landmark mansion, which is the centerpiece of the campus. Photographic credit: Maxwell Mackenzie.

New Corporate Offices in San Francisco

As the rage for blue jeans grew in the 1970s, so did the fortunes of Levi Strauss & Co. As sales grew, the company relocated its corporate headquarters to a high-rise office tower in its hometown of San Francisco, California. But the restrictions of high-rise corporate life chaffed at the hierarchy and employees of the company who had prided themselves on maintaining a family sense in their business affairs. The company teamed with a local developer to build a new corporate home in which the familial relationships that the company knew best could once again be nourished.

The new corporate headquarters, called Levi's Plaza, is still located in San Francisco at the base of Telegraph Hill facing the Embarcadero. The new corporate home is a campus setting of four new office buildings combined with the renovation of the former Italian Swiss Colony Warehouse and another brick warehouse on a four block area. The new buildings house the management functions of the company. The major entrance into the company headquarters is through an atrium framed in blue-painted steel to echo the denim blue of the company's most famous product.

The buildings surround (and are surrounded by) parks, plazas, streams, and waterfalls that offer an urban retreat. The park and plaza areas with their animated water elements evoke memories of the "water course in the Sierras" where the company's products were first introduced. Throughout the complex, there are views and vistas out to the Bay and up Telegraph Hill. The new buildings are set back with the rise of each floor creating numerous balconies that offer spectacular views.

Levi's Plaza in San Francisco, California is the new corporate home of Levi Strauss & Company whose most famous product is blue jeans. The plan for the new corporate offices consciously included parks, plazas, streams, and waterfalls. Photographic credit: Peter Aaron, Esto Photography.

CREDITS
NAME & LOCATION: Levi's Plaza, San Francisco, California
ARCHITECTS FOR NEW BUILDINGS: Hellmuth, Obata and Kassabaum, Inc., St. Louis, Missouri
ARCHITECTS FOR THE INTERIOR AND RENOVATIONS: Gensler & Associates, San Francisco, California
LANDSCAPE ARCHITECT: Lawrence Halprin, San Francisco, California
DEVELOPER: Jim Joseph, Gerson Bakar and Al Wilsey in conjuction with The Equitable Life Assurance Society, San Francisco, California

The office building features set backs on each floor creating balconies that offer spectacular views of the city and the harbor. Photographic credit: Peter Aaron, Esto Photography.

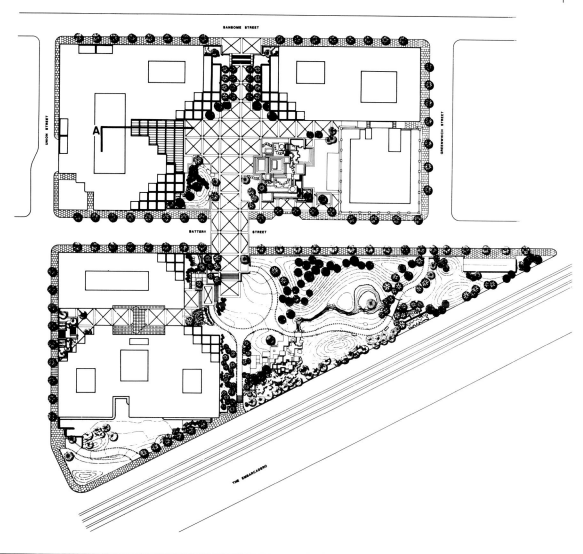

The Levi Strauss offices are spread out in a campus-like setting over a four block area.
Drawing credit: Hellmuth, Obata and Kassabaum.

Mid-Block Court Provides Urban Amenities

In the old section of Philadelphia, Pennsylvania five unrelated buildings on the same block have been adaptively reused as an apartment complex with ground floor commercial space. A center court that had previously functioned as the service alley for the buildings has been turned into a landscaped entry for the project. The courtyard serves as the single entry point for the complex and all circulation, including the elevator, occurs via the courtyard. The courtyard itself is connected to the street by a covered passageway. Not only does the courtyard provide increased security for residents of the complex, but it also allows light and air to reach apartments that face onto the courtyard.

In Philadelphia, Pennsylvania, five unrelated buildings in the city's old section have been adaptively reused as a new apartment development. The buildings have been united by a new landscaped center court created out of a former service alley. The center court serves as the single entry point into the complex, and all circulation within the complex occurs through the court. Photographic credit: James B. Abbott.

CREDITS
NAME & LOCATION: *Bank Street Court, Philadelphia, Pennsylvania*
ARCHITECT: *Elliot J. Rothschild, AIA, The Rothschild Company/Architects, Philadelphia, Pennsylvania*
DEVELOPER: *Historic Landmarks for Living, Inc.*

Urban Design Considerations Paramount in Adaptive Reuse of Fire Station

The 1880s Keystone Firehouse and adjacent buildings are a prominent landmark marking a gateway intersection into downtown Reading, Pennsylvania. The redevelopment plan for these buildings called for commercial and retail uses of the structures. The urban design elements of the streetscape of Reading were a major determinant in the design approach for the project. The existing historic buildings were rehabilitated, and incompatible twentieth-century structures on the site were demolished. New construction maintained the scale of the streetscape. The new and the old were tied together by creating a major new entrance to the project from the street and by a carefully defined color scheme. The entrance is defined by a trellis behind which is an off-street parking facility.

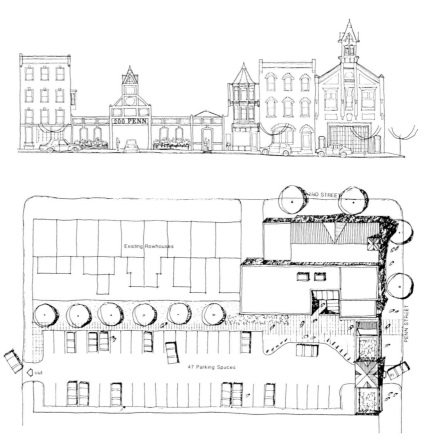

Retail and commercial activities are located in these revitalized historic buildings at a central location in Reading, Pennsylvania. An important element of the overall plan is the entrance to the complex marked by a trellis-like structure that maintains the street scale. Parking is located behind the entrance and includes a pedestrian drop-off point for access to the complex. Drawing credit: The Rothschild Company/Architects.

CREDITS
NAME & LOCATION: *The Keystone Firehouse, Reading, Pennsylvania*
ARCHITECT: *Elliot J. Rothschild, AIA, The Rothschild Company/Architects, Philadelphia, Pennsylvania*
DEVELOPER: *Heritage Investment Group, Reading, Pennsylvania*

Siting a Classic Arts Center

In 1958 the Wellesley College Arts Center, designed by Paul Rudolph, was completed after nearly two years of study of the needs of the college and the proposed location of the new building at the center of the college campus. The major issues, as defined by Rudolph, were (1) major buildings were sited on the hills overlooking the valleys, (2) buildings are grouped in clusters forming courtyards with coherent landscaped outer spaces, but the distances between the clusters are unimpeded, and (3) the buildings have elaborate vertical silhouettes. In developing the plan for the new college Arts Center, Rudolph followed these principles.

The Arts Center is located on a high point of the hill on a retaining wall. As the site flows downward toward the valley, it encompasses the music and drama building. A large outdoor stairway in a courtyard focuses on a Gothic tower that marks the center of the campus. The materials and design of the Arts Center are consciously intended to evoke the architectural imagery of the various architectural styles and vocabularies of the other campus buildings.

CREDITS
NAME & LOCATION: Mary Cooper Jewett Arts Center, Wellesley College, Wellesley, Massachusetts
ARCHITECT: Paul Rudolph, Architect, New York, New York
ASSOCIATED ARCHITECT: Anderson, Beckwith & Haible
STRUCTURAL ENGINEER: Goldberg, LeMessurier Associates

The Wellesley College Arts Center in Wellesley, Massachusetts was designed by Paul Rudolph and completed in 1958. The design of the structure emerged from a careful study of the existing relationships carried out by Rudolph. The building, located on a prominent hill, flows down toward a valley and echoes the architectural styles of the surrounding campus buildings. Photographic credit: Mark Feldberg.

New Building Contributes to Park Renaissance

Druid Hill Park is a city park near downtown Baltimore, Maryland. As part of a planned revitalization of the park, the city has undertaken the expansion of the existing conservatory on the site. The new building, which will add 18,000 square feet of interior space to the existing 3,000 square feet, is in an H-shape plan and attempts to echo and blend with the existing conservatory,

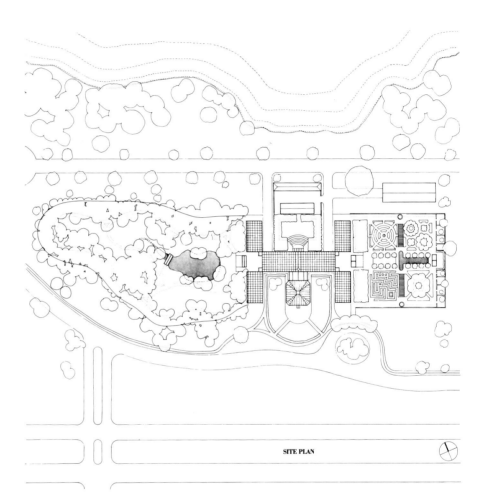

SITE PLAN

The revitalization plan for Druid Hill Park in Baltimore, Maryland includes a new 18,000-square foot building to complement the existing historically designated conservatory. As part of the revitalization effort, two new gardens will be constructed on either side of the conservatory. One will be a formal classic garden, and the other will be an informal romantic garden. Drawing credit: Cass and Pinnell Architects.

CREDITS
NAME & LOCATION: The William Donald Schaefer Conservatory and Gardens, Druid Hill Park, Baltimore, Maryland
ARCHITECT OF RECORD: Sulton Campbell & Associates, Baltimore, Maryland
DESIGN ARCHITECT: Cass and Pinnell Architects, Washington, D.C.
HISTORIC PRESERVATION: Walmsley & Co., Inc., New York, New York
LANDSCAPE ARCHITECTS: Graham Landscape Architects, Annapolis, Maryland
STRUCTURAL ENGINEERS: Light & Space Associates, Ltd., New York, New York
MECHANICAL ENGINEER: Goldman Copeland Batlan & Oxman, New York, New York
DEVELOPER: City of Baltimore, Department of Parks and Recreation

The new conservatory will surround the existing orangerie in a carefully planned urban park landscape. Rendering: William Gaffney.

which is listed on the National Register of Historic Places. A new orangerie will provide additional room for new plant types, an amphitheater, as well as additional exhibition space and a new terrace. The plan includes construction of a formal classic garden on one side of the conservatory and an informal romantic garden on the other. Space in the new complex will be available for outdoor lectures and concerts, as well as public and private social functions.

One-Story Building Transformed into Alternative School Facility

In the Old City Hall Historic District of Tacoma, Washington, an abandoned and derelict former garage-like structure has been reworked to become a contributing part of the historic district. The small-scale structure was flanked by taller late nineteenth- and early twentieth-century buildings. The front facade of the building faced onto a principal thoroughfare, but had been

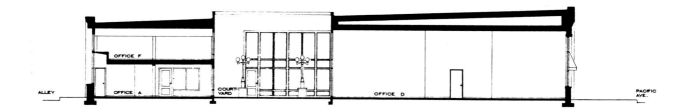

Bodega Court is a new office building in Tacoma, Washington that was created out of a derelict garage-like structure. The principal facade of the building, which is located in a historic district, had been completely obliterated as a result of a number of previous remodeling efforts. A new facade, modeled on the existing rear elevation, is compatible with the existing architecture in the historic district. Drawing credit: Alan Liddle.

CREDITS
NAME & LOCATION: *Bodega Court, Tacoma, Washington*
ARCHITECT: *Alan Liddle, FAIA, Tacoma, Washington*

A central courtyard was created in the center of the small-scale structure to provide access through the building and to bring sunlight into the interior of the building. Photographic credit: Gary Vannest Photography.

completely obliterated during the various uses of the building. There was no documentation of its original appearance.

A new facade, which recalls the brick facade on the alley side of the building, was designed in harmony with the historic district and the surrounding buildings. An outdoor courtyard was created in the center of the building to provide both air and light to offices on the interior of the 125-foot long building, as well as a stairway for egress to office space on the second floor. The building is currently being used by a private organization that provides alternative schooling to high school dropouts.

The Middlesex County Courthouse complex in East Cambridge, Massachusetts was begun in 1814, and a number of additions were added during the next century and a half. By 1970, the county court system had completely outgrown the facilities, new quarters were constructed, and the historic courthouse complex was slated for demolition. Photographic credit: Richard Cheek.

CREDITS
NAME & LOCATION: Bulfinch Square, Cambridge, Massachusetts
ARCHITECT: Graham Gund Architects, Cambridge, Massachusetts
DEVELOPER: Bulfinch Square Limited Partnership

Courthouse Complex Escapes Demolition to Become Multiuse Facility

The former Middlesex County Courthouse in East Cambridge, Massachusetts was built in 1814 and designed by Charles Bulfinch. The courthouse was added onto and expanded several times throughout the nineteenth century, most notably by Ammi B. Young in 1848. In 1901 additional courthouse buildings were built surrounding the original building. But by 1970 the Middlesex County court system had completely outgrown the facilities; new facilities were constructed in 1973, and the original structures were slated for demolition for a parking lot.

A reuse scheme saved the complex, which is now home to the Cambridge Multicultural Arts Center as well as other offices. The Arts Center uses the steps of the old courthouse as seating for a performance amphitheater. Photographic credit: Steve Rosenthal.

However, the complex was listed on the National Register of Historic Places and has been totally rehabilitated as a multiuse facility. A number of former courtrooms have become theater, gallery, and workshop space for the Cambridge Multicultural Arts Center, and other space has been turned into modern offices.

The uses of the interior spaces are imaginative and thoughtful, and the landscaped outdoor spaces around the complex have been unified to serve a number of purposes. The portico on the nineteenth-century facade of the courthouse and the landscaping surrounding the building have been restored using documentary evidence from a nineteenth-century lithograph. This outdoor space is now tied to the Lechmere Canal Park System. An outdoor performance amphitheater for the Arts Center will use the steps of the old Superior Courthouse for seating. The project is complex, but makes use of imaginative urban design solutions combined with careful attention to the restoration and rehabilitation of the existing buildings on the site.

Southwest Army Arsenal Turned into Corporate Headquarters

In San Antonio, Texas a former army arsenal constructed in 1858 has been transformed into the headquarters of the H. E. Butt Grocery Company, a major food chain in south Texas. Portions of the arsenal complex are listed on the National Register of Historic Places. The project combines renovation

The new headquarters for a major food chain in San Antonio, Texas is a former army arsenal contructed in 1858. Historic portions of the arsenal, which is located on the San Antonio River, were reused together with new construction to create an office campus. Photographic credit: Peter Aaron, Esto.

CREDITS
NAME & LOCATION: H.E. Butt
   Grocery Company
   Corporate Headquarters,
   San Antonio, Texas
ARCHITECT: Hartman-Cox Architects,
   Washington, D.C.
ASSOCIATED ARCHITECT: Chumney/
   Urrutia, San Antonio, Texas
LANDSCAPE ARCHITECT: James E.
   Keeter, San Antonio, Texas
DEVELOPER: H.E. Butt Grocery
   Company, San Antonio, Texas

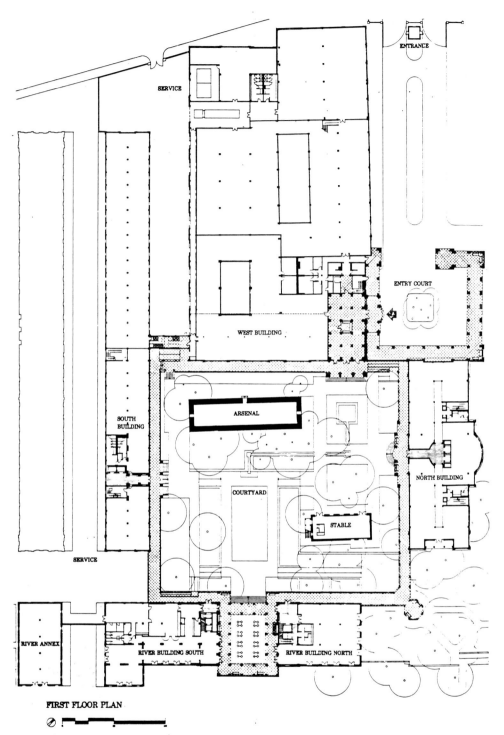

ENTRANCE

SERVICE

ENTRY COURT

WEST BUILDING

ARSENAL

SOUTH
BUILDING

COURTYARD

NORTH BUILDING

STABLE

SERVICE

RIVER ANNEX

RIVER BUILDING SOUTH

RIVER BUILDING NORTH

FIRST FLOOR PLAN

*The company's office campus is oriented toward the adjacent river, and the buildings
are sited to provide views to the river. The entrance to the complex is via a driveway
flanked by gateposts that are reminiscent of a typical southwestern army post.
Drawing credit: Hartman-Cox; Chumney/Urrutia, associated architects.*

of some of the existing structures with new construction to create an office campus for the firm's headquarters.

The project, located on the San Antonio River, involved the selective demolition of a number of structures and the total rebuilding of two buildings together with the construction of one new building to create a four-building complex centered around a large courtyard. The courtyard, designed to provide a respite for company employees, contains trees, grass, gravel walkways, limestone fountain, and generous areas for sitting and rest.

The rehabilitated buildings have porticoes and terraces that provide views of the adjacent river. All of the buildings in the complex are connected by wide-covered walkways. The architecture combines the traditional southwestern Texas architecture with that of a typical Army post. The entrance to the complex is through a gate with an articulated driveway that terminates in an entry court. The low scale of the buildings respects the neighboring architecture of the historic district across the river.

12

The Missing Tooth: New Infill Construction

Like a dentist to a boxer, architects and developers are finding more opportunities to work with the missing teeth of urban architecture. Gaps in a city's streetscape—whether caused by man, such as a parking lot between two buildings, or by nature, such as a fire that levels a row house—that are filled in by the construction of new buildings constitute an important area of concern in mixing old and new buildings. Such construction, called infill construction, "fills in" or completes a streetscape by making use of unused or underused sites, usually by sharing common walls with adjacent buildings.

Although the infill building can function separately, such as a single-family row house on a residential block, it is often used as a connector between two buildings or to fill in a vacant space of one larger building. It is this concept of the building itself as the connector to complete the streetscape or fill in the vacant area of a larger building that presents designers of infill construction with a challenge.

By combining an infill building with an existing building, a number of amenities can be created that will enhance the new complex. For example, infill construction offers the opportunity to create a new lobby or entrance for the building; a roof deck or an interior atrium or courtyard can also be added. But the design and construction of infill structures are often more complicated than freestanding buildings because the connections with existing systems, often much older, are cause for careful detailing.

Infill buildings have been the subject of great interest to historic preservationists for years. For example, the development around Lafayette Park, across Pennsylvania Avenue from the White House in Washington, D.C., is composed of a number of infill structures designed to be compatible with the existing early nineteenth-century residential structures. The infill buildings were designed by John Carl Warnecke and Associates during the 1960s as part of a larger complex of federal government office space. They maintain the residential and pedestrian scale of the park, while the larger office buildings are set back from the park and create, in effect, a visual wall that separates the residential feeling of the park from the surrounding city.

Infill construction can have both historic and economic value. Properly designed, it can complete a streetscape using either vacant or underused land. The architect is challenged with designing a new building in close proximity to older buildings, often adding visual distinction. In many cities, where downtown development is booming, small parcels of land or vacant air space offer the only alternatives for development.

Sites used for infill structures are often deemed undesirable: the site may have poor drainage, or the rights to the site may be tied up in litigation, or the owner may not agree with a developer on price. In such instances, at the time of initial development, the site is simply bypassed and nothing is built. A potential infill site can also be created by an event that destroys the original building, such as a fire.

The development surrounding Lafayette Square directly across the street from the White House in Washington, D.C. is composed of a number of infill structures designed to be compatible with the existing historic nineteenth-century townhouses. The infill buildings were part of a larger complex of federal government office space constructed during the 1960s. Photographic credit: Peter H. Smith.

A small sliver of available land on Connecticut Avenue near the White House in Washington, D.C. was filled in with an office structure between two larger developments. Photographic credit: Peter H. Smith.

Often in urban areas such vacant lots or sites become surface parking lots, allowing the owner to generate some income from the site while awaiting appropriate development. An infill structure creates a more intensive use of the land than a parking lot.

The development of a potential infill site must be carefully approached. The reasons that a site was originally bypassed during the initial development phase are often powerful, and can continue to be valid reasons to prevent further development. For example, changes in land topography and drainage problems may be the principal reasons that a site has remained undeveloped. Before tackling an infill development project, the history of the site should be understood to know the reasons for the lack of development.

There are a number of generalized rules that should be adhered to in the design of infill structures so that they are compatible with their neighbors. Scale of the new infill building is the most important consideration. An analysis of the dominant or major visual features and characteristics of the existing streetscape should be undertaken before beginning design work on an infill building. This analysis should include information on features such as height, building materials, stylistic characteristics of buildings, color, and window rhythm.

The development of an infill building also presents challenges to the designer as a number of extremely important practical considerations come into play. If the infill building is to be connected to its neighboring buildings to form a complex, the jurisdiction's fire and building code requirements for the existing buildings may change. As a result of the new construction, the existing buildings may have to meet new code requirements.

In cases in which the infill buildings are physically attached to the adjacent buildings, the adjacent buildings will, in most cases, have to be underpinned or shored up to protect them during the construction process. Similarly, careful structural consideration will also have to be given to the manner in which the outside walls are joined. In some instances, it may be possible to use the walls of the adjacent buildings as an integral part of the structural system of the infill building. In other cases, the infill building will have to be built as an independent structure that has no structural integration with the adjacent buildings. The space contained in an infill structure can become a part of or an extension of the space available in the neighboring buildings. Particular attention needs to be paid to floor levels in such instances.

In cases in which the infill building becomes an extension of the adjacent buildings, HVAC and other mechanical/electrical systems can be consolidated into one area of the building allowing the creation of more useable floor space for tenant use. Infill space can also be used for lobbies, courtyards, atriums, or circulation space.

Rowhouse Residence, Washington, D.C.

One of the best known examples of infill construction in historic areas is a rowhouse in the Georgetown historic area of Washington, D.C. built in 1968. The building displays all the characteristics that are indicative of sensitive infill construction. It conforms to the prevailing height of the other structures in the row, it is similar in scale to its neighboring buildings, its windows resemble those found in nearby houses, and the material—brick—is the predominant building material in most of Georgetown.

The building does not, however, simply copy the neighboring buildings. It is clearly a modern interpretation of the architectural characteristics of the nineteenth-century streetscape. It has won a number of design awards.

Police and Fire Station

In New York City, a combination police and fire station, built in the late 1880s, required expansion and upgrading of its facilities to meet the modern demands for these essential city services. The original buildings were part of a row of four late nineteenth-century public buildings. The architects for the expansion used an existing gap in the middle of the row to insert 63,000 square feet of new space while preserving the visual links that connect the row structures.

Except for the facades of the existing buildings, everything was demolished and replaced with new construction. To provide column-free floor space on the lower floors and to minimize risk to the historic buildings, perimeter columns were used to support three long-span trusses on the fifth and sixth floors from which the lower floors were suspended. Once the connection was

An early example of residential infill construction in a historic district is this rowhouse in the Georgetown area of Washington, D.C. Built in 1968, the structure conforms in materials, height, window rhythm, and other design characteristics of the area. Photographic credit: Peter H. Smith.

CREDITS
NAME & LOCATION: Residence, Washington, D.C.
ARCHITECT: Hugh Newell Jacobsen, FAIA, Washington, D.C.

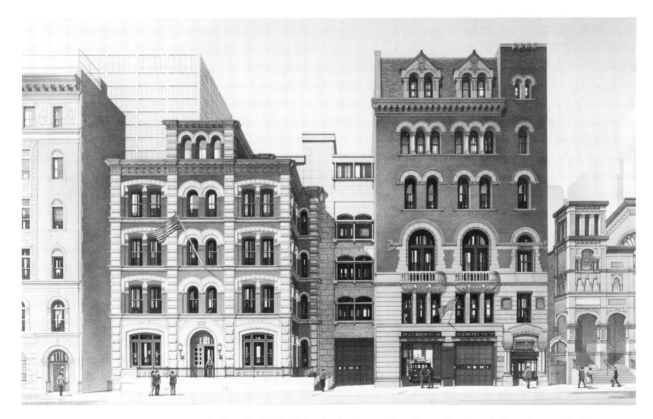

In New York City, late nineteenth-century fire and police stations, housed in two separate buildings, were combined using infill construction between and behind the existing structures. The infill portion of the project uses materials that match those of the original structures. Drawing credit: The Stein Partnership.

CREDITS
NAME & LOCATION: Combined Facility for 19th Precinct and Engine Co. 39 and Ladder Co. 16, New York, New York
ARCHITECT: The Stein Partnership, New York, New York
DEVELOPER: The City of New York

made between the new building and the upper floors of the existing structures, the new floor levels were added in sequence from the upper to the lower floors.

The addition is set back from the street line of the police and fire stations. The materials of the original structures—brick and granite—were used as the primary facade materials in the new infill section. In addition, the openings on the rear and side elevations of the new section were detailed in brick to match the historic style of openings in the original structures. Much of the original stone work on the historic buildings was deteriorated due to spalling and flaking. As needed, deteriorated stone on the historic facades was replaced with new cast stone material duplicated from molds of the original stonework.

To make the building more energy efficient, up to 70 percent of the building's lighting requirements are met through the use of windows and skylights. Windows are operable in the new building, an old idea whose time is returning.

Small Building Infill

In Newtown, Pennsylvania two former residences were joined with an ingenious small infill structure to allow their conversion into law offices. One building was a stone residential building constructed in the late eighteenth century; the other was a brick residential-scale building with a storefront built in the mid-nineteenth century. The buildings were separated by a small yard between them.

The architects designed an addition to the larger stone residential structure and then developed a light, airy arcade to provide access between the two buildings. The arcade is the infill element of the ensemble and, because of its design, similar to a porch of almost any period, provides a smooth transition between the two strikingly different styles of residential architecture.

A small infill structure joins two former residential structures in Newtown, Pennsylvania. The arcade provides access between law offices now located in the two structures. Photograhic credit: Short and Ford, Architects.

CREDITS
NAME & LOCATION: Law Offices, Newtown, Pennsylvania
ARCHITECT: Short and Ford Architects, Princeton, New Jersey
DEVELOPER: Sidney Yates, Esq.

Torpedo Factory

On the waterfront in Alexandria, Virginia one of the buildings of a former torpedo factory built in 1918 and once operated by the U.S. Navy became home to a colony of artists' studios in 1974. The imaginative adaptive reuse quickly became a popular tourist attraction amid the other tourist sites of the eighteenth-century port city. As the Alexandria Art Center grew haphazardly, both in its physical home and as a tourist destination, it became apparent that a revitalization program for the remainder of the other buildings on the site would contribute substantially to the local economy of the city and serve as a more secure link between the historic downtown and the waterfront along the Potomac River.

CREDITS
NAME & LOCATION: Torpedo Factory, Alexandria, Virginia
ARCHITECTS: Metcalf and Associates/Keyes Condon Florance, Architects, Arthur Keyes, Principal-in-Charge, Washington, D.C.

In 1974, a former torpedo factory on the waterfront of Alexandria, Virginia had become home to a colony of artists' studios. As part of an overall revitalization scheme for the complex, infill construction was undertaken to provide retail space, restaurants, and a boat club. Photographic credit: Maxwell MacKenzie.

In 1978, the city sponsored a development/design competition that proposed virtually rebuilding the existing building of the former torpedo factory complex as well as developing two new structures at one end of the complex to house retail and restaurant facilities and the restoration of the docks and piers on the river side of the complex.

The infill components of the project added several important elements to the project and provided needed amenities. The retail market is sheathed in glass to stress its relationship to the large window areas of the former factory complex. The restaurant and boat club are conceived of in a Victorian shingle style.

Two 2-Family Rowhouses

Zoning Requirements
Min. Lot Area: 1600sf
Proposed: 1610sf & 1630sf
Max Coverage: 50 %
Proposed: 42% & 50%
Req'd Parking: 1 Space/Unit
Proposed: 4 Spaces
Est. Construction Cost:
$310,000

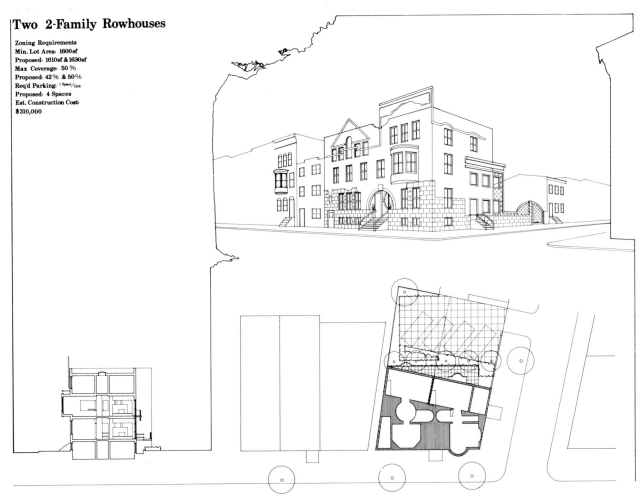

A national competition for the design of infill buildings was held by Historic Albany of Albany, New York. The competition, won by Martin & Jones Architects of Washington, D.C., was for infill residential structures for a historic section of the city. The project was not built. Drawing credit: Martin & Jones Architects.

CREDITS
NAME & LOCATION: *Infill Housing Design Competition, Albany, New York*
ARCHITECT: *Martin & Jones Architects, Washington, D.C.*
COMPETITION SPONSOR: *Historic Albany, Inc., Albany, New York*

Infill Competition

In 1981 Historic Albany, a city-wide preservation organization in Albany, New York, sponsored an innovative design competition. The competition was specifically to develop an infill design solution for two vacant residential lots in a historic section of the city directly across the street from the New York State Governor's Mansion. The fact that a local preservation organization chose to sponsor a national design competition specifically for infill structures dramatically points out how important infill design and construction are considered.

The design that was selected was praised for its responsiveness to the design elements in the surrounding neighborhood. Although Historic Albany was certainly innovative in conducting such a focused design competition that emphasized an increasingly difficult preservation issue, the organization was not as adept at the management of design competitions. The competition offered no cash prize to the winner, but rather title to the building lots and the right to build the winning design on the lots. Because of a number of issues, the winning design was never built.

Addition to Landmark Downtown Club

The Metropolitan Club is a venerable institution located in downtown Washington, D.C., a block and a half from the White House. The building, a designated Washington landmark, was subject to considerable regulatory and design review for a project that added 20,000 square feet to the existing 55,000 square feet of space in the historic structure. The expansion was required for additional space for athletic, dining, service, and administrative offices.

The designers were faced with the challenge of integrating the mechanical, electrical, plumbing, and structural systems of a new building with those of the existing structure. In addition, new fire stairs and an elevator system were added. The infill addition is located between the club building and an existing

The next door neighbor of the Metropolitan Club, Washington, D.C. is a speculative curtain wall office building. Photographic credit: Robert Katz.

CREDITS
NAME & LOCATION: *Metropolitan Club, Washington, D.C.*
ARCHITECT: *Bowie-Gridley Architects, Washington, D.C.*
STRUCTURAL ENGINEER: *James M. Cutts and Associates*
MECHANICAL/ELECTRICAL ENGINEERS: *Summer Consultants, Inc.*

speculative office building. The addition is very respectful of the original architecture of the landmark building and incorporates balustrades, pilasters, and fenestration that nearly replicate original design elements. The addition also uses materials similar to those used in the historic building.

Infill Office Complex on Pennsylvania Avenue

The Apex Building has long been a significant visual landmark along Pennsylvania Avenue about halfway between the Capitol and the White House. A twin-turreted building, originally designed as a hotel in 1860, was renovated in 1888 by Alfred Mullett, supervisory architect of the U.S. Treasury, to serve as a bank. The Apex Building is reported to be one of the earliest examples of fire-safe construction in Washington. In later years, the building housed the Apex liquor store. The Apex Building, along with two adjacent buildings,

As part of the redevelopment scheme for Pennsylvania Avenue in Washington, D.C., two historic buildings located adjacent to each other were slated for preservation. An infill structure between the two buildings, the twin turreted Apex Building and the former studio of Civil War photographer Mathew Brady, serves as the connecting link between the two structures and houses mechanical equipment, elevators, and fire stairs so that the historic buildings could be preserved. Photographic credit: Arnold Kramer.

CREDITS
NAME & LOCATION: Sears House, Washington, D.C.
DESIGN ARCHITECT: Hartman-Cox Architects, Washington, D.C.
ARCHITECT: Geier Renfrow Brown (Phase I); Leo A. Daly (Phase II), Washington, D.C.
PRESERVATION ARCHITECT: John Milner Associates
DEVELOPER: Sears, Roebuck and Co., Washington, D.C.

one of which had served as the studio for Civil War photographer Mathew Brady, were targeted for preservation and reuse by the Pennsylvania Avenue Development Corporation.

The project involved the revitalization of the two buildings together with new infill construction to connect them. Together, the new project provided approximately 45,000 square feet of office space for the operations offices of the Sears World Trade organization. The conceptual architects for the project developed a scheme that made use of an alleyway for an infill structure to house elevators, mechanical systems, and fire stairs so that space in the historic buildings would not be destroyed. The new infill structure's design derives from the original exterior elements of the Apex's design and serves as a connecting element between the two halves of the project. The project was awarded a preservation citation by the Washington Metropolitan Chapter of the American Institute of Architects.

CREDITS
NAME & LOCATION: Church Court Condominiums, Boston, Massachusetts
ARCHITECT: Graham Gund Architects, Cambridge, Massachusetts

In 1978 the historic 1892 Mount Vernon Church in Boston's Back Bay area was destroyed by fire. The remains of the church have been combined with new infill construction to create a residential condominium complex. Photographic credit: Steve Rosenthal.

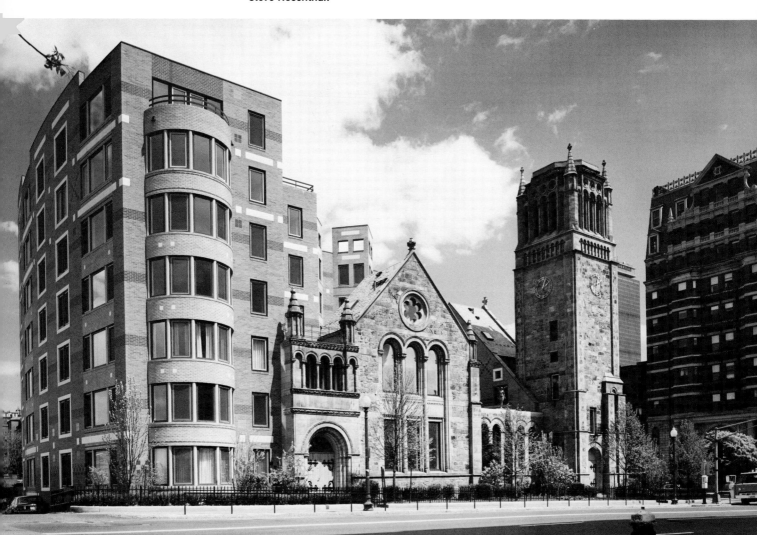

Destroyed Church Developed as Condominiums

In 1978 the Mount Vernon Church, located in Boston's Back Bay area, was destroyed by fire. Designed by the Boston architectural firm of Walker and Kimball in a vibrantly Richardsonian fashion, it was completed in 1892. All that remained after the fire were the central bell tower and portions of two entrances. In 1979 the remains of the church, together with the adjacent parish house, were purchased by a developer.

The ruins of the church and the extant parish house were combined with new infill construction to create a total of 40 condominium units. The complex, known as Church Court, was hailed by Boston architectural critic Robert

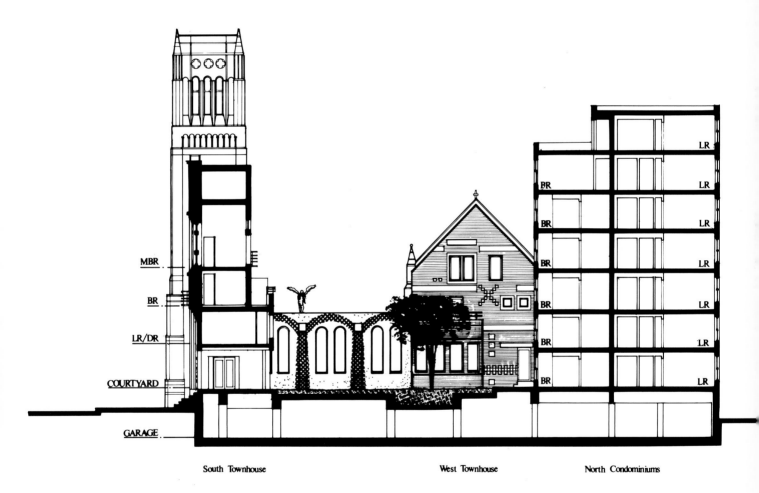

South Townhouse West Townhouse North Condominiums

SECTION A-A

The remaining walls of the church were retained as a backdrop to an interior courtyard, a new seven-story structure was added, and one unit was created in the surviving church bell tower. Drawing credit: Graham Gund Architects.

A group of nineteenth-century commercial structures in Washington, D.C.'s arts district has been developed as retail and office space including art galleries. Originally there were five buildings. As part of the redevelopment program, an infill structure was built on the site of one of the buildings that had previously been destroyed. The design of the infill structure contrasts with that of the historic buildings and houses mechanical equipment for the other buildings in a common core. The new structure also allows for circulation throughout the complex by providing steps to compensate for the grade changes within the site. Photographic credit: Peter Aaron, Esto.

CREDITS
NAME & LOCATION: *Gallery Row, Washington, D.C.*
DESIGN ARCHITECT: *Hartman-Cox Architects, Washington, D.C.*
PRESERVATION ARCHITECTS: *Building Conservation Technology and Oehrlein and Associates, Washington, D.C.*
DEVELOPER: *Carley Capital Group and Gallery Row Associates, Washington, D.C.*

Campbell as "the most influential new piece of architecture in Boston since the Hancock Tower. . . ."[1]

The original walls of the ruined church serve as a backdrop to an interior courtyard. Wrapped around the courtyard are the condominium units, which include a seven-story element. The design idioms of the new condominiums derive from the neighborhood design elements found in the surrounding blocks of Back Bay. Both the brick of the new elements and its color are sympathetic to the area. The project has won a number of architectural design awards and was singled out by *TIME* magazine as one of the 10 best designs of the year in 1983.

Gallery Row

In the Seventh Street arts district of Washington, D.C. four retail structures were rehabilitated under the revitalization plans of the Pennsylvania Avenue Development Corporation. Gallery Row was originally a row of five structures when built during the latter part of the nineteenth century—one of the structures was earlier destroyed.

Under the developer's plans, the buildings were to be restored to their original uses—as retail and office space. But on detailed structural inspection, the buildings were found to be severely affected by adjacent subway construction. The facades, in some instances, were separated by as much as 6 inches from the rest of the building. It was determined that the buildings had deteriorated far too much to be saved in place.

The preservation architects devised a plan to dismantle the facades of the buildings and then reerect them, stone by stone, on a new core structure.

Elevation shows five original buildings with new infill connecting structure. Drawing credit: Hartman-Cox Architects.

[1] Robert Campbell, "Church Ruins Wall Condominiums," *Architecture*, May 1985.

Following reconstruction of the buildings, the pieces of the facade that had been catalogued were reattached in the original configuration to recreate the original appearance. Stonework that could not be reused was replaced by new precast concrete pieces that were molded from original pieces.

To provide continuous circulation through the 36,000-square foot project, a new common core to house elevators, fire stairs, and mechanical equipment was designed as a new infill building in place of the structure that had been destroyed. This new building, while using many of the design elements common in the older buildings in the row, is clearly modern in design.

In contrast to the stone facades of the original historic buildings, the infill building makes expansive use of glass in its facade. Because the site slopes considerably from one end of the row to the other, the new infill building is used as a means of changing the grade level within the interior of the project by allowing a short series of steps to compensate for the differences in elevation between the ends of the row. The project was recognized with an award from the Washington Metropolitan Chapter of the American Institute of Architects.

Index to Professional Firms

Amar Consulting Engineers, 165
Amman & Whitney, New York, New
    York, 138
Anderson, Beckwith & Haible, 180

Bentel & Bentel Architects, Locust
    Valley, New York, 53
Beyer Blinder Belle, New York, New
    York, 138
Bohlin Powell Larkin Cywinski, Wilkes-
    Barre, Pennsylvania, 90, 120, 141
Boston Architectural Team, Inc., Chelsea,
    Massachusetts, 58, 60
Bowie-Gridley Architects, Washington,
    D.C., 173, 197
Brunner/Cott & Associates, Inc.,
    Cambridge, Massachusetts, 41, 42,
    76, 77
Bryant & Bryant, Washington, D.C., 23
Building Conservation Technology,
    Washington, D.C., 161, 202
Burley Partnership, The, Waitsfield,
    Vermont, 99
Burt Hill Kosar Rittelman Associates,
    Pittsburgh, Pennsylvania, 141

CAD-CON, Inc., 173
Cambridge Seven Associates, Inc.,
    Cambridge, Massachusetts, 95
Cannon, Inc., Buffalo, New York, 100,
    124
Cass and Pinnell Architects, Washington,
    D.C., 181
Chumney, Jones & Kell, Inc., San
    Antonio, Texas, 95
Chumney/Urrutia, San Antonio, Texas,
    186
Cohen-Barreto-Marchertas, Inc., 165
Cutts, James M., and Associates,

Washington, D.C., 197

Daly, Leo A., Washington, D.C., 199
Design Concepts, Inc., Sioux Falls, South
    Dakota, 32
Dotter Engineering, Inc., 141

Eskew Vogt Salvato & Filson, Architects,
    New Orleans, Louisiana, 56

Geddes Brecher Qualls Cunningham
    Architects, Philadelphia,
    Pennsylvania, 147
Gensler & Associates, San Francisco,
    California, 175
Gilley-Hinkel Architects, Bristol,
    Connecticut, 86
Goldberg, LeMessurier Associates, 180
Goldman Copeland Batlan & Oxman,
    New York, New York, 181
Graham Landscape Architects,
    Annapolis, Maryland, 181
Grier Renfrow Brown, Washington, D.C.,
    33, 199
Gund, Graham, Architects, Cambridge,
    Massachusetts, 184, 200

H.W.H. Associates, Denver, Colorado, 30
Haines Lundberg Waehler, New York,
    New York, 114
Halprin, Lawrence, San Francisco,
    California, 175
Hardy Holzman Pfeiffer, New York, New
    York, 13
Hartman-Cox Architects, Washington,
    D.C., 7, 9, 153, 159, 186, 199, 202
Hastings + Chivetta, 79
Hellman, Harold H., FAIA, Architect,
    Chicago, Illinois, 103, 105, 107

205

Hellmuth, Obata & Kassabaum, Inc.: St. Louis, Missouri, 121, 129, 175 Washington, D.C., 163
Holabird and Root Architects, Chicago, Illinois, 18, 165
HTB, Inc., Oklahoma City, Oklahoma, 21, 87, 122

ICON, Washington, D.C., 162

Jacobsen, Hugh Newell, FAIA, Washington, D.C., 140, 193
James Architects and Engineers, Inc., Indianapolis, Indiana, 97
Johnson, Carol R., & Associates, Cambridge, Massachusetts, 110

Kaplan/McLaughlin/Diaz, San Francisco, California, 56, 117, 118
Kaye, Samuel H., Architect, Columbus, Mississippi, 8
Keeter, James E., San Antonio, Texas, 186
Keyes Condon Florance Architects, Washington, D.C., 22, 23, 69, 195
Koubek, Vlastimil, Washington, D.C., 13

Liddle, Alan, FAIA, Tacoma, Washington, 183
Light & Space Associates, Ltd., New York, New York, 181

McCartney Lewis Architects, Washington, D.C., 11
Martin & Jones Architects, Washington, D.C., 47, 135, 149, 196
Metcalf and Associates, Washington, D.C., 195

Milner, John, Associates, 199
Mitchell/Giurgola, 79
Monahon, Richard M., Jr., AIA, Peterborough, New Hampshire, 98, 136, 139
Moore, Arthur Cotton, FAIA, Washington, D.C., 127
Moriyama & Teshima, Toronto, Ontario, 165

Nagle, Hartray & Associates, Ltd., Chicago, Illinois, 70, 103
Navy, Marshall & Gordon Architects, Washington, D.C., 153
Notter Finegold + Alexander, Boston, Massachusetts, 110

Oehrlein & Associates, Washington, D.C., 28, 159, 161, 202

Pappageorge/Haymes Ltd., Chicago, Illinois, 72

Roche, Kevin, John Dinkeloo and Associates, Hamden, Connecticut, 31
Rothschild Company/Architects, The, Philadelphia, Pennsylvania, 50, 51, 54, 62, 151, 170, 178, 179
RTKL Associates, Inc., Baltimore, Maryland, 89
Rudolph, Paul, Architect, New York, New York, 180

Schwartz, Robert, Washington, D.C., 49
Sharratt, John, Associates, Inc., Boston, Massachusetts, 44, 74
Short and Ford Architects, Princeton, New Jersey, 46, 112, 194

Skidmore, Owings & Merrill: Chicago, Illinois, 83, 105, 107 Houston, Texas, 12 Washington, D.C., 152
Smith, Segreti & Tepper, Washington, D.C., 159
Souza, True & Partners, Boston, Massachusetts, 110
Spiegel and Zamecnik, Washington, D.C., 99
Spitznagel, Architects, Engineers, Planners, Sioux Falls, South Dakota, 109
Stein Partnership, The, New York, New York, 193
Sulton Campbell & Associates, Baltimore, Maryland, 181
Summer Consultants, Inc., 197

Taft Associates, Houston, Texas, 43, 80
Team Four, St. Louis, Missouri, 79
Thompson, Benjamin, FAIA, Boston, Massachusetts, 127
Thompson Consultant, Inc., Marion, Massachusetts, 100
Thompson Engineering Co., Inc., Boston, Massachusetts, 110

Utility Engineers, 90

Walmsley & Co., Inc., New York, New York, 181
Warnecke, John Carl, & Associates, Washington, D.C., 163
Winsor Faricy Architects, 118

Zeidler Roberts Partnership, Toronto, Ontario, 115

Subject Index

Accessibility, 93, 95, 98, 109, 113, 171
Acoustical, see Interiors
Adler and Sullivan, 79, 124
Additions, 88, 106, 109
   abstract, 15–24
   appreciative, 3–14
   contrasting, 15–24
     style of architecture, 15
   imitative, 25–34
   sheds, 100
   tower, 86
   wraparound, 17
Alabama, Birmingham, 146
Alabama Power Company
   Headquarters, 146
Albany, New York, 197
Alexandria, Virginia, 132
   Alexandria Arts Center, 195
   Torpedo Factory, 195
All Saints Church, 139
Alleyway, 200
Alteration, 35
Alumni Center, University of
   Michigan, 141
Ann Arbor, Michigan, 141
Apex Building, 198
Arcade, 194
Architect of the Capitol, 134
Architectural style, 146
   Art Deco, 21, 146, 172
   Art Moderne, 69
   Beaux-Arts, 4, 6, 7, 16, 17, 22, 66,
     122, 154
   chateau, 31
   classical, 17, 143
   Colonial, 132
   eclectic, 98, 148, 154, 196
   Federal, 6, 8, 77
   Georgian Revival, 11, 17, 134, 172

   Gothic Revival, 26, 63, 86, 101, 109,
     121, 122, 137
   Mediterranean, 29
   Mission, 137
   Romanesque, 33, 48, 61, 94, 201
   Second Empire, 12
   shingle, 98
   Spanish Revival, 55
Armory, 28
Arsenal, 186
Atlantic Coastline Building, 160
Atrium, 21, 43, 45, 59, 66, 68, 70,
   79, 101, 115, 116, 119, 127,
   146, 164, 175
Arts center, 28, 93, 180, 186, 195
Attic, 110
Auditorium, 98, 105, 123
   stage, 106

Balcony, 116, 119
Baltimore, Maryland:
   Druid Hill Park, 181
   Mercantile Safe Deposit and Trust
     Building, 158
   Schaefer, William Donald,
     Conservatory and Gardens, 181
   USF&G Mount Washington Center, 88
Bank, 22, 57, 78, 134, 158
Bank Street Court, 177
Barn, 53, 100
Basement, 85, 100
Basking Ridge, New Jersey, 113
Bathroom, 121
Beldeden, 85
Bethesda, Maryland, 172
Birmingham, Alabama, 146
Blackstone Falls, 41
Blake, Moffitt, and Towne Building, 116
Bodega Court, 182

Bonfils Mansion, 29
Boston, Massachusetts:
  Boston Public Library, 17
  Burberry House, 76
  Charles Street Meeting House, 73
  China Trade Center, 119
  Church Court Condominiums, 201
  Mercantile Wharf Building, 44
  Piano Craft Guild Housing for Artists,
    38
  San Marco/Lincoln Wharf, 59
Boston Globe, 131
Boston Public Library, 17
Boylston Building, 119
Brady, Mathew, 200
Brewery, 93, 94
Bridge:
  footbridge, 137
  pedestrian, 94
  vehicular, 137
Bristol, Connecticut, 85
Brooks Museum of Art, 12
Buffalo, New York:
  Erie Community College, 101
  Goldome Bank for Savings
    Corporate Headquarters, 158
  Guaranty Building (Prudential
    Building), 124
Building Additions Design, 1
Bulfinch, Charles, 185
Bulfinch Square, 185
Burberry House, 76
Burberry's, 152
Burnham, Daniel, 134

California:
  Palo Alto, 137
  San Francisco, 55, 116, 174
Cambridge, Massachusetts:
  Bulfinch Square, 185
  Cambridge Multicultural Arts
    Center, 186
  North and Cabot Houses, Radcliffe
    Quadrangle, Harvard
    University, 110
Cambridge Multicultural Arts Center,
  186
Campbell, Robert, 131, 201
Campus, *see* Colleges and universities
Carbery School Building, 38
Carnegie Mellon University, 141
Carriage house, 11
Cartney-Hunt House, 8
Castle Center for the Arts, 28
Cathedral of Learning, 143
Ceiling:
  dropped, 57, 65
  height, 49, 53, 102, 123
Central Falls, Rhode Island, 41
Central High School, 122
Charles Street Meeting House, 73
Chicago, Illinois:
  Chicago Historical Society, 17
  Manufacturers Hanover Plaza, 167
  Newberry Library, 7

116 South Michigan Avenue, 71
Twenty North Michigan Avenue, 70
University of Chicago:
  Goodspeed Hall, 106
  Leon Mandel Assembly Hall, 105
  Walker Museum/Graduate School
    of Business, 102
Chicago Historical Society, 17
Chicago Municipal Building, 71
China Trade Center, 110
Chinese Economic Development
  Council, 119
Chocolate Works, The, 171
Chrysler, Walter, 9
Chrysler Building (New York), 172
Chrysler Museum, 9
Church, 48, 139, 201
Church Court Condominiums, 201
Churn, 65
Circulation, 4, 43, 52, 73, 95, 102,
  113, 115, 203
City Hall, 49
Civil Engineering Landmark, 129
Clocktower, 137
Club, 197
Cluss, Adolph, 154
Cobb, Henry Ives, 7, 102, 106
Codes:
  building and life safety, 40, 68,
    101, 192
  seismic, 55
  variance, 63
Colby-Sawyer College, 100
Colleges and universities: 96, 100,
  101, 102, 105, 106, 110, 137,
  141, 163, 180
  campus, 88
Color, 16, 22, 27, 82, 179
Colorado, Denver, 29
Columbus, Mississippi, 8
Combined Facility for 19th Precinct
  and Engine Co. 39 and Ladder
  Co. 16, 192
Competition, design, *see* Design
  competition
Connecticut, Bristol, 85
Connector, 15, 17, 189
Conservatory, 181
Construction (new):
  freestanding, 133–144
  attached, 145–155
Contextualism, 131
Convent, 55
Corridor, 92
Courthouse, 185
Courtyard, 53, 55, 57
  exterior, 83, 155, 177, 180, 184,
    188
  interior, 148, 163, 203
Cows, 100
Cret, Paul, 7
Crown and Eagle Apartments,
  42
Crown and Eagle Mills, 42
Curtain wall, 83, 143, 146

Dallas, Texas, 82
Dallas Morning News, 82
Davenport, Evans, Hurwitz & Smith
  Building, 32
Davies, William, 172
Decatur Carriage House, 11
Delaware Aqueduct, 137
Delaware River, 137
Demonet Building, 152
Department of Defense, 141
deSibour, Jean Henri, 154
Design Center (Washington, D.C.), 24
Design competition, 79, 128, 134,
  153, 196, 197
Denver, Colorado, 29
DePauw University, 96
Detailing, architectural, 24, 29, 77,
  94, 134, 152, 198
Dibner, David R., 1
Dibner-Dunlap, Amy, 1
Dillon, David, 82
District of Columbia, *see* Washington,
  D.C.
Don't Tear It Down, 164
Door, 17
Driveway, 188
Druid Hill Park, 181
Dublin, New Hampshire, 98
Dublin School, Main House, 98

East Capitol Car Barn, 46
East College, DePauw University, 96
Elderly Housing, *see* Residential
Electrical equipment, *see* Mechanical/
  electrical equipment
Elevator, 61, 70, 73, 95, 119
  exterior tower, 33, 79
  grillage, 125
Emily Morgan Hotel, 121
Encore Condominium Redevelopment,
  29
Energy use, 194
Entrance, 12, 17, 19, 52, 53, 57, 71,
  73, 78, 85, 92, 100, 109, 110,
  120, 134, 148, 155, 179
  automobile, 171
  pavilion, 143
Erie Community College, 101
Evans, Oliver, 113
Event, space, 116, 119, 128
Exteriors, 22. *See also* Facade
  brick, 24, 33, 41, 79, 148, 184,
    192
  brownstone, 33
  cleaning and repair, 27, 90,
    98
  corner, 160
  glass, 163
  masonry, 94
  mirror glass, 24
  oxidation, 82
  setback, 175, 194
  stucco, 29, 59
  terra cotta, 71, 86, 124
  walls, 203

Facade. 157–168
    replacement. 66. 203
    restoration. 120
Factory. 38. 119. 171. 195
Faith Baptist Church. 48
Federal offices. *see* Office space
Festival marketplace. 128. 129
Fire station, 160, 179, 192
First American Bank Building, 22
Fleming, Ronald Lee, 172
Floor, 94
    levels, 192, 194
    new, 102
Folger Shakespeare Library, 7
Fred Harvey Restaurant, 130
Freestanding construction, *see*
    Construction (new), freestanding

Gallery Row, 203
'Galveston, Texas:
    Springer Building, 42
    Hendley Building, 80
Galveston Historical Foundation, 82
Garage, *see* Parking
Garden, 182
George Washington University, 163
Gift Center, The, 116
Gilbert, C.P.H., 31
Goldberger, Paul, 35
Goldome Bank for Savings Corporate
    Headquarters, 158
Goodhue, Bertram, 4
Goodspeed Hall, 106
Greenbrier Resort, 11
Greencastle, Indiana, 96
Greenhouse, 172
Greyhound Bus Terminal, 69
Guaranty Building (Prudential
    Building), 124
Guernsey Hall, 113
Guthrie, George W., School, 90
Gymnasium, 172

H.E. Butt Grocery Company
    Corporate Headquarters, 186
Haas, Richard, 43
Handicapped, *see* Accessibility
Hardenbergh, Henry, 12
Harrisburg, Pennsylvania, 49
Harrisburg Old City Hall, 49
Hardy Holzman Pfeiffer, 12
Harkness Tower, Yale University,
    26
Height, 192. *See also* Zoning
Hendley Building, 80
Heurich Mansion, 33
Hill, James G., 160
Historic Albany, Inc., 197
Historical Society of Washington,
    D.C., 33
Holabird & Roche, 167
Hotel, 11, 12, 121, 130
Hospital, 32, 55, 109
HVAC, *see* Mechanical/electrical
    equipment
Hyattsville, Maryland, 28

Illinois, Chicago, 7, 17, 70, 71, 102,
    105, 106, 167
Indiana, Greencastle, 96
Infill construction, 110, 189–204
Institutions, 93–110
InterFirst II Building, 82
Interiors, 40, 51, 59, 111–130
    acoustical, 52, 106, 107
    features, 111, 113, 121, 123
    layout, 113
    partitions, 90
    setback, 70
    technology, 111
    upgrading, 45, 63, 66, 111, 113, 119
    walls, 98, 101
InterMetro Industries Corporation
    Headquarters, 90
International Market Square, 119
Institute for Museum Services, 128
Italian Swiss Colony Warehouse, 174

Jefferson Hotel, 154
Jewett, Mary Cooper, Arts Center, 180
Jewish Museum, 31
Johnson/Burgee Architects, 17
Julia Place, 55

Keystone Firehouse, 179
Kidder, Tracy, 134
Koubek, Vlastimil, 12

Laboratory, 143
Lackawaxen, Pennsylvania, 137
Lafayette Park, 189
Landscape, 40, 42, 46, 109, 186
    preservation, 169
Latrobe, Benjamin Henry, 11
L'Enfant, Charles Pierre, 152
Levi Strauss & Co., 174
Levi's Plaza, 174
Library, 7, 17, 100, 106
Lighting, 68, 172, 194
Link, Theodore C., 128
Loading area, 68, 106
Lobby, 68, 69, 71, 73, 78, 83, 102,
    119, 125, 148, 163
Location, 38
Lone Star Brewery, 94
Longworth House Office Building, 65
Louisiana, New Orleans, 55
Low income housing, *see* Residential

McAuley Hall, 88
McKim, Mead and White, 17
Madison National Bank Building, 134
Magruder School, 154
Mandel Assembly Hall, 105
Mansion, *see* Residential
Manufacturers Hanover Plaza, 167
Martin & Jones, 46
Maryland:
    Baltimore, 88, 158, 181,
    Bethesda, 172
    Hyattsville, 28
Massachusetts:
    Boston, 17, 38, 44, 59, 73, 76, 119,

    201
    Cambridge, 110, 185
    New Bedford, 77
    Uxbridge, 42
    Wellesley, 180
Massing, 134, 160
Materials, building, 4, 16, 133, 134,
    137, 146, 180. *See also* Exterior
    bricks, 27, 109, 141, 146, 194
    concrete, 17, 143
    granite, 17, 71, 82, 141, 194
    limestone, 71, 109, 141, 143
    masonry, 143
    stone, 27, 160, 194
Means, Mary, 157
Mechanical/ electrical equipment
    (HVAC), 4, 21, 27, 29, 49, 57,
    68, 95, 98, 192
    air conditioning, 21
    ductwork, 52
    heat pump, 29, 113
    integration, 197
    water turbine, 41
Mechanicsburg, Pennsylvania, 61
Medical Arts Building, 121
Medical building, 121
Mellon Institute, 143
Memphis, Tennessee, 12
Mercantile Building, 44
Mercantile Safe Deposit and Trust
    Building, 158
Mercantile Wharf Building, 44
Metropolitan Club, 197
Michigan, Ann Arbor, 141
Microclimate, 169
Mid-Continent Building, 86
Mid-Continent Tower, 88
Middlesex County Courthouse, 185
Mill, 37, 38, 41, 42, 51, 113
Millrace, 113
Minisink, New York, 137
Minneapolis, Minnesota, 119
Mississippi, Columbus, 8
Missouri, St. Louis, 79, 128
Moore, Alfred F., Factory, 51
Mount Vernon Church, 201
Moynihan, Daniel Patrick, 124
Mullet, Alfred, 198
Multiuse facility, 186, 196
Munsingwear Factory, 119
Mural, 43
Museum, 9, 12, 17, 31, 33, 93, 94,
    102, 113, 123, 154

National Academy of Sciences, 4
National Endowment for the Arts, 128
National Endowment for the
    Humanities. 128
National Park Service, 128, 137
National Press Building, 66
National Register of Historic Places,
    35, 61, 86, 119, 121, 122, 129,
    172, 181, 186
National Trust for Historic
    Preservation, 11, 79, 157
New Bedford, Massachusetts, 77

New Hampshire:
  Dublin, 98
  New London, 100
  Peterborough, 134, 139
New Jersey:
  Basking Ridge, 113
  Princeton, 45, 113
New London, New Hampshire, 100
New Orleans, Louisiana, 55
New York:
  Albany, 197
  Buffalo, 101, 124, 158
  Minisink, 137
  New York City, 31, 137, 192
  Oyster Bay Cove, 53
New York, New York:
  Combined Facility for 19th Precinct
    and Engine Co. 39 and Ladder
    Co. 16, 192
  Jewish Museum, 31
  Trinity Church Overpass, 137
Newberry Library, 7
Newtown, Pennsylvania, 194
Norfolk (Virginia) Museum of Arts
  and Sciences, 9
North and Cabot Houses, Radcliffe
  Quadrangle, Harvard University,
  110

Office space, 21, 32, 65–92, 102, 113,
  115, 119, 122, 125, 134, 143,
  146, 148, 152, 155, 159, 161,
  163, 167, 174, 184, 186, 188,
  194, 203
  electronically enhanced, 65
  federal, 68, 101, 128, 134, 190
  upgrading, 66
Oklahoma:
  Oklahoma City, 21, 122
  Tulsa, 86
Oklahoma City, Oklahoma:
  One Bell Central, 122
  Robinson Renaissance Building, 21
Old Post Office (Washington, D.C.),
  68, 127
One Bell Central, 122
116 South Michigan Avenue, 71
1001 Pennsylvania Avenue, 159
1100 New York Avenue, 69
1752 N Street, N.W., 148
1911 Pennsylvania Avenue, N.W., 162
Ontario, Toronto, 115
Orangerie, 182
Oyster Bay Cove, New York, 53

Palo Alto, California, 137
Parish Hall, 139
Park, 181, 189
Park Hill, 55
Park Road Apartments, 57
Parking, 40, 53, 55, 66, 78, 88, 92,
  109, 139, 170, 179, 191
  driveway, 170
  garage, 151, 182
Pedestrian access, 171
Pennsylvania:
  Harrisburg, 49

Lackawaxen, 137
Mechanicsburg, 61
Newtown, 194
Philadelphia, 51, 171, 177
Pittsburgh, 53, 141, 151
Reading, 179
Wilkes-Barre, 90
Pennsylvania Avenue Development
  Corporation, 12, 200, 203
Perrine Building, 21
Peterborough, New Hampshire:
  All Saints Church, 139
  Peterborough Savings Bank, 134
Philadelphia, Pennsylvania:
  Bank Street Court, 177
  Chocolate Works, The, 171
  Wireworks, The, 51
Photogrammetry, 161
Piano Craft Guild Housing for Artists,
  38
Pittsburgh, Pennsylvania:
  School House, The, 151
  Shadyside Commons, 53
  Software Engineering Institute, 141
Plaza, 20, 79, 120, 143, 172
Plumbing, 59
Police station, 192
Portico, 186
Post Office, 68, 101, 127
Power plant, 29
Princeton, New Jersey:
  Guernsey Hall, 113
  2 Library Place, 45
Public art, 171

Queen's Quay Terminal, 115

Radcliffe Quadrangle, 110
Reading, Pennsylvania, 179
Red Lion Row, 163
Remaking America, 35
Renaissance Tower, 82
Residential, 8, 29, 37–64, 73, 98,
  113, 115, 134, 151, 171, 177,
  192, 201
  dormitory, 106, 110
  elderly housing, 41, 42, 57
  low income housing, 59
  mansion, 29, 33, 45, 85, 113, 172
  townhouses, 148, 162
Restaurant, 51, 78, 116, 128, 130
  dining hall, 110
Retail, 22, 42, 44, 55, 57, 70, 73, 76,
  83, 115, 119, 128, 129, 152,
  164, 179, 203
Review board, 25, 132, 133, 162, 165
Rhode Island, Central Falls, 41
Riggs Bank Building, 25, 57
Robinson Renaissance Building, 21
Roche, Kevin, 32
Rodman Candleworks, 77
Roebling, John A., 137
Roof, 48
  lines, 141
  slate, 90
  tile, 29
Rogers, James Gamble, 12

Rudolph, Paul, 180

St. Joseph's Hospital, 55
St. Louis, Missouri:
  Union Station, 128
  Wainwright State Office Building,
    79
St. Paul's Cathedral, 143
San Antonio, Texas
  Emily Morgan Hotel, 121
  H.E. Butt Grocery Company
    Corporate Headquarters, 186
  Museum of Art, 93, 94
San Antonio Museum of Art, 93, 94
San Francisco, California:
  Gift Center, The, 116
  Levi's Plaza, 174
  Park Hill, 55
San Marco/Lincoln Wharf, 59
Scale, 16, 17, 137, 146, 148, 188,
  191
Schaefer, William Donald,
  Conservatory and Gardens, 181
School, 38, 49, 61, 90, 98, 122, 151,
  153, 172, 184
School House, The, (Mechanicsburg,
  Pennsylvania), 61
School House, The, (Pittsburgh,
  Pennsylvania), 151
Sears House, 198
Sears World Trade organization, 200
Security, 69, 177
Sessions, William E., 85
Sessions Mansion, 85
Shadyside Commons, 53
Shepley, Rutan and Coolidge, 105
Site and urban design, 169–188, 190
  trapezoidal, 155
  topography, 172, 180
Sioux Falls, South Dakota:
  Davenport, Evans, Hurwitz & Smith
    Building, 32
  Veterans Administration Hospital,
    109
Skidmore, Owings & Merrill, 12, 82
Skylight, 61, 92, 101, 116, 123, 194
Skyscraper, 124
Small, Smith and Webb, 11
Software Engineering Institute, 141
South Dakota, Sioux Falls, 32, 109
Southwestern Bell, 122
Springer Building, 42
Stabilization, 158, 161
Stable Arts Center, 93
Stair tower, 32, 52
Staircase, 125
Stairway:
  enclosed, 68, 92
  exterior, 180, 184
  open, 68, 98, 102, 113
Stanford Memorial Church, 137
Stanford University, 137
Star-Spangled Kitsch, 26
Steadman, David, 9
Sterner, Frederick Junius, 11
Storefront, 125, 194
Street furniture, 172

Streetscape, 179, 189, 190
Structural system, 40, 102, 167, 192
  buttress, 80, 158
  columns and trusses, 192
  connection, 146
  deterioration, 80, 98
  engineering, 158
  integration, 197
  roof, 83
  steel frame, 61, 76, 80, 107
  wood frame, 52
Sumner School, 154
Sumner Square, 153
Susan-Colgate Cleveland Library,
  Colby-Sawyer College, 100

Tacoma, Washington, 182
Tennessee, Memphis, 12
Terminal Hotel, 130
Texas:
  Dallas, 82
  Galveston, 42, 80
  San Antonio, 93, 94, 121, 186
Theater, 111
Time Magazine, 203
Topography, *see* Site and urban
  design
Toronto, Ontario, 115
Toronto Terminal, 115
Torpedo Factory, 195
Tower Group of Buildings, 105
Townhouses, *see* Residential
Train Station, 128
Transportation access, 170
Tregaron, 172
Trellis, 92, 179
Trinity Church Overpass, 137
Trolley barn, 46
Tulsa, Oklahoma, 86
Twenty North Michigan Avenue, 70
2 Library Place, 45
2000 Pennsylvania Avenue, N.W., 163

U.S. Capitol, 25
Union Station (St. Louis), 128
University, *see* Colleges and
  universities

University of Chicago:
  Goodspeed Hall, 106
  Leon Mandel Assembly Hall, 105
  Tower Group of Buildings, 105
  Walker Museum/Graduate School of
    Business, 102
University of Michigan, 141
University of Pittsburgh, 141
USF&G Mount Washington Center, 88
Uxbridge, Massachusetts, 42

Van Dorn Mill, 113
Veterans Administration Hospital, 109
Virginia, Alexandria, 132

Wainwright Building, 78
Walker and Kimball, 201
Walker Museum/Graduate School of
  Business, 102
Walkway, 22, 52, 53, 137, 139, 188
Walls, *see* Exteriors; Interiors
Warburg Mansion, 31
Warehouse, 24, 42, 44, 53, 55, 70,
  80, 115, 116, 146, 160, 174
Warnecke, John Carl, and Associates,
  190
Washington, D.C., 134, 146
  Atlantic Coastline Building, 160
  Carbery School Building, 38
  Decatur Carriage House, 11
  Demonet Building, 152
  East Capitol Car Barn, 46
  Faith Baptist Church, 48
  First American Bank Building, 22
  Folger Shakespeare Library, 7
  Gallery Row, 203
  Historical Society of Washington,
    D.C., 33
  Lafayette Park, 189
  Longworth House Office Building,
    65
  Madison National Bank Building,
    134
  Metropolitan Club, 197
  National Academy of Sciences, 4
  National Press Building, 66
  Old Post Office, 68, 127
  1001 Pennsylvania Avenue, 159

1100 New York Avenue, 69
1752 N Street, N.W., 148
1911 Pennsylvania Avenue, N.W.,
  162
Park Road Apartments, 57
Riggs Bank Building, 25
Rowhouse residence, 192
Sears House, 198
Stable Arts Center, 93
Sumner Square, 153
2000 Pennsylvania Avenue, N.W.,
  163
U.S. Capitol, 25
Washington Design Center, 24
Washington International School,
  The, 172
Willard Inter-Continental Hotel and
  the Willard Office Building, 12
Washington, Tacoma, 182
Washington Design Center, 24
Washington International School, The,
  172
Weese, Harry and Associates, 7
Wellesley, Massachusetts, 180
Wellesley College, 180
West Virginia, White Sulphur Springs,
  11
White, George, 134
White Sulphur Springs, West Virginia,
  11
Wilkes-Barre, Pennsylvania, 90
Willard Inter-Continental Hotel and
  the Willard Office Building, 12
Window, 17, 19, 44, 63, 65, 68, 192
  arched, 29
  double glazed, 90, 120
  frame, 95
  new, 61
  operable, 194
  replacement, 57
  rhythm, 151
  wall, 20
Wireworks, The, 51

Young, Ammi B., 185

Zoning, 22, 55, 113, 133, 158, 172
  height, 152, 155, 159